PLAY AND GAMES

Mitchell Beazley

PLAY AND GAMES

CONTENTS

Moyra Austin

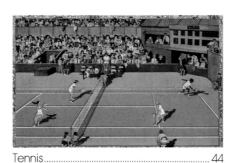

THE ARTISTS

LET'S LEARN

LANGUAGE AND EDUCATION CONSULTANT

Professor Peter Herriot
Birkbeck College, University of London

LEARNING SKILLS ADVISER

Dr. Sara Meadows
Department of Education
University of Bristol

PLAY AND LEARN ADVISER

Peter Dixon
King Alfred's College, Winchester

ADVISORY PANEL

Gill Barnet
Maxilla Day Nursery Centre, London

Lesley Chandler
Edmund Waller Infants' School, London

Jan Cooper
Centre for Urban Education Studies
Inner London Education Authority

Marion Dowling
Infant and Pre-School Education Adviser
Dorset Education Authority

Joyce Jurica
Centre for Language in Primary Education
Inner London Education Authority

Janet O'Connel
Inner London Pre-School Playgroups Association

Pam Smith
Department of Psychology, Hatfield Polytechnic

John Stannard
Primary Education Adviser
Inner London Education Authority

Joanna Studdert
Centre for Urban Education Studies
Inner London Education Authority

ISBN 0 85533 429 0

LET'S LEARN

About this series

Young children learning

Children start exploring their world before they can even speak and long before they reach school. You can see their understanding develop by watching the things they do and, as they begin to learn to talk, you can actually hear it because they do much of their thinking aloud either by talking to themselves, or by questioning adults and other children.

Children and adults

During these early years, children do not separate their day into times for learning and times for playing; they learn all the time as they play. This means that the adults who spend most time during the day with a child can enormously assist that child's learning if they treat answering and posing questions as fun, if they go at the child's pace and, perhaps above all, if they spend time talking and doing things together.

Learning by talking

The *Let's Learn* books are planned not only to give you the pleasure that all families get from sharing good books but also to present a wide range of information in specially designed pictures that will encourage your child to talk about them and so come to understand them fully. Time and again you will find your child looking at a picture of a scene he recognizes and seeing far more in it as he talks with you. As he does so, you will notice that your child is gradually acquiring a wider vocabulary and learning to speak more fluently. This, rather than early mastery of mechanical skills, is the vital key to your child's development in the early years. Children who talk fluently master other intellectual skills more easily.

Children gaining skills

The *Let's Learn* books offer a balanced range of early learning skills which will develop all sides of your child's thinking. By practising these skills in ways that will be easy and enjoyable for both of you, you will give your child the start he needs into activities such as reading, calculating, problem solving and logical reasoning, and therefore provide him with a firm foundation which teachers, and others, can build on as he grows older.

Asking questions

The best way to answer a child's question is often to ask another one. By doing so, you can help your child to sort out what he already knows and help him to use that information to begin to answer his own question. If your child seems interested in an idea but can't answer your question, think about how you have asked it. Does he clearly understand what you mean? It's not always easy to rephrase a question so that you are asking the same thing in a simpler way, but you can sometimes make a game of trying to do so. Asking questions that children can't answer is not a clever way to stretch their thinking, but a sure way to confuse them; so, if they really don't know the answer, tell them.

Age range

The *Let's Learn* books are designed for use with children between the ages of three and six. At three your child will already be passing from the simple identification of objects in a picture that many two-year-olds can manage – eg "there's a boat" – and will be ready to work out exactly what is happening in quite complicated pictures. By the time he is six, your child will be quite capable of understanding most of the more advanced ideas that lie behind some of the pictures as well as spotting all the more intricate details.

Terminology

Throughout the text, "younger" and "older" have been used to indicate either end of the three to six range. However, all young children vary enormously in what they can do and how they think and it is impossible to be precise about which child will be able to manage any particular task. Because you will be doing most of this work with one child, children have usually been referred to in the singular and "he" and "she" have been used equally. All the exercises and suggestions are appropriate for children of either sex.

Pace

Children will vary enormously in how much time they want to spend on any one picture, in how often they want to look at it again and in how much more they find to talk about on their second and third looks. It is important not to go too fast. Give your child plenty of time to think round an idea, question you and come up with his own suggestions. Try to stop working on a picture before your child (or you) is bored by it. When you come back to it later, you will find that your child wants to spend longer on it and understands the ideas behind it more fully.

8 Around the World
EXPLORING OUR WORLD
Climbing Hills

Children's answers to the question "Why do we climb hills" are much the same as the answers an adult mountaineer will give you – because they're there; they're fun; they're a challenge. This picture introduces themes that come up again later in the volume (see p. 28).

☐ Climbing can be hard work. You often need to use your arms as well as your legs to help push you up the hill.
☐ Once you have climbed to the top you can see how quickly you can get to the bottom of the hill again.
☐ Going down is quicker and easier than climbing up.
☐ Sand dunes make good places for early climbing adventures. We all do things like climbing or jumping for the first time when we are ready to. Children should not force others to climb or jump when they don't feel confident.

Picture points
1 That girl has already reached the top of the sand hill. She is holding a flag to show that she is "king of the castle".

2 There are different ways of climbing. Look at the girl who is not managing very well. She is not using her arms to help her. Some children find it easier to climb up on their hands and knees. That boy is climbing up the other side, so we can only see his head.

3 It's much slower climbing up the hill than it is sliding down, especially on sand because your feet sink into it.

4 If you are brave you can jump from the top of this hill. The sand is nice and soft to land on.

5 That boy doesn't want to join in the game. He prefers watching the ships out at sea. Why did he climb the hill?

Using The Pictures

The text is organized in a logical order that follows the way most children will approach a picture. They are likely to want to scan it and work out what is going on, then come to talk more generally about it and then be interested in the associated learning skills. However, your child may prefer to start with one of the activities in the back of the book and you should usually let him start where he wants to.

Main Ideas

1 The italic type tells you why the picture is included in the volume while the points immediately below outline the main ideas behind it. Most of these ideas will seem startlingly obvious, but children need to think gradually about things that adults often take for granted. When you first look at a picture together, let your child talk about it in his own words for as long as he wants to. (This may only be for a few minutes with younger children.) Try to follow up the comments that seem likely to lead to further talking. The main text is written in a style that young children can follow if you simply read it to them; it is even better if you can adapt the text and have an entirely natural chat.

Picture Points

2 Check through the picture points and talk about any parts of the picture that have not already been mentioned. This may give you the chance to help your child to identify new objects or introduce new ideas. There are suggested answers (in brackets) to many of the questions to show what you can reasonably expect from your child, but remember that a child's logic may produce all sorts of ideas and it is always worth finding out the thinking behind an apparently illogical answer.

Climbing Hills 9

Talking Points

1 We can climb on different things. You climb on the climbing frame in the park. What other things can people climb? (Stairs, ladders, trees, etc.)

2 What makes it hard to climb a hill? (How steep it is, how slippery it is.)

3 Do you think the other children mind being pushed down by the "king of the castle"? Would you mind? Can you explain how to play? Do you know the words that the king calls out?

Learning Skills

Sand play
Sand, like water, is magic to children. Nobody would want to spoil the pure fun they have with it, but as they get older you can help them to think constructively about the things they have already found out in play.
□ (Pour dry sand into the top half of an old detergent bottle.) Look, it trickles through the nozzle. Let's see what patterns we can make by pouring sand on the ground.
□ Could you run upstairs and back before all the sand empties out? (Older children may time other activities in "bottles of sand".)
□ What happens if we pour some water on to sand? (It sticks together.) Then what can we do with it? Could you make sandcastles with dry sand?
□ Sand pours when it's dry and sticks together when it's wet, so what is it made of? (Lots and lots of tiny bits. Older children may be able to tell you a lot more about those bits by using a magnifying glass.)

What people are doing
Talk about all the different actions that are shown in the picture. Use a variety of action words while you are doing this.
□ That's a steep hill made of sand. Show me the people who are climbing up. Which are using their hands to climb as well as their feet? Why? Can you think of a word which describes that way of climbing? (Scrambling.) Who's going faster, the scramblers or the girl who's trying to walk up?
□ Who is sliding down the hill? Who is jumping down the hill? Who is already at the bottom? Who is standing on top of the hill and looking out to sea?
Story and games on p.51

Talking Points

3 The talking points provide appropriate conversation topics; try to have a good conversation rather than accepting, or giving, one-word answers. You will need to listen as well as talk, ask as well as answer questions, make jokes and, at all stages, remind your child of experiences you have already shared which relate to the ideas in the picture. When children are really interested in a subject, they are likely to go on asking questions about it at times when you are not expecting them. Although it is not always easy to be alert to this, do try to respond with a positive answer that shows you know what they are thinking about and that you are interested in their ideas.

Learning Skills

4 Practise the Learning Skills whenever your child is interested. There are two different skills on each page: the first one is usually easier than the second. The italic type at the head of each section advises you on the purpose of each exercise and the questions in each section usually go from easier to harder. Ask the questions your child can answer, come back to the more difficult ones on another occasion. The skills on each page are the ones that are most appropriate for that picture and the books have been planned so that all skills are practised at different levels. Once you are used to introducing learning skills, you will find that you can practise most of them with any of the pictures. When you first look at the suggestions for learning skills you may think that your child has already mastered them; for instance, that he knows what all the colours are. You will soon realize, however, that children can have a certain amount of knowledge without a great deal of understanding. Enjoyable practice that goes carefully over each step is the way to increase his understanding and make him feel confident about learning.

PLAY AND GAMES

About This Book

Playing and learning

It's easy to call most of the things young children do all day "play". It may not seem very important to us but it is vital for them. When they are playing, they are learning. It is their opportunity both to try things out and to start relating to other children.

Playing together

Whenever people play together, all sorts of unspoken social rules are involved. Children don't always understand these properly and they need to talk about them with you so that they can come to get on well with their friends and play successfully.

Keeping rules

As children grow older, they begin to take part in many forms of recreation and to play complicated games with increasingly demanding rules. Learning to keep rules is, of course, a vital part of all children's development. This book is organized to help you to talk about them at both simple and quite advanced levels. It often seems that children pick up the rules of a game from their friends, but questioning can reveal that rules learned in this way have not been properly understood.

Physical skills

Although you are likely to notice when children acquire new physical skills, they usually develop them without thinking very hard about it themselves. You can help older children to gain confidence and increase skills by practising with them, by setting small challenges and by watching and commenting on expert players or performers with them. One thing that children seem to know almost instinctively is when they are ready to attempt a new challenge and they should not be forced.

Playing alone

Playing games together is all part of being a family but there are times when children need to play with their friends or on their own. Your role then may simply be to see "fair play", or stand by to give ideas when needed. This is especially important when children are playing imaginative games. It's their game, not yours, so let them get on with it.

Main Themes

In addition to giving information and ideas, this book is organized in six sections which follow a developing theme. Younger children will be too busy coming to grips with all kinds of information to notice this but you may find that older children are ready to start thinking in broader terms.

Children's Play

Young children start playing by themselves but soon start learning to play alongside others and gradually to co-operate with them.

Imaginative Play

Imaginative games are always enjoyable. They also often help children to talk about themselves and their predicaments in ways that do not inhibit them.

Early Rules

As children start to play games together they need to learn that rules are important. If they break them, they risk spoiling everybody's enjoyment.

Keeping Rules

More complicated games have formal rules that have to be kept if the game is to succeed. The referee is an extremely important figure.

Music And Dance

Some recreational activities can be very enjoyably developed through hard work, practice and team work. Children are excited by such performances long before they have acquired the skills involved themselves.

Physical Skills

As children develop their physical skills, they can perform at higher levels and come to appreciate the experts.

Key Ideas

□ People often play successfully on their own.

□ Some games need teams.

□ Enjoyable imaginative play is immensely valuable for all children.

□ Most games have winners and losers.

□ Everybody has to keep the rules because breaking them spoils the game.

□ People like watching games played by experts.

In The Sandpit

Children and sand go together naturally, but a few helpful suggestions can make all the difference between desultory pie-making and much more imaginative play.

☐ There are all kinds of things you can do with sand. You can make patterns with it, build with it, pour it and dig it.

☐ If you pour water on sand, the grains all stick together.

☐ Sand gets everywhere; it gets in your clothes and shoes.

☐ Children often like to play alone, but it is still good to have others around.

Picture points

1 Do you know the names of all the things the children are using in their sandpit?

2 The rake makes good curving lines, doesn't it? What else could you use to make lines and patterns?

3 Can you see the moulds the boy used to make the shapes? What else did he press into the sand?

4 The sieve has holes in the bottom and the boy is shaking the sand through the holes. What might be left in the sieve at the end? (Stones, twigs.) Why?

5 The little girl isn't very good at making sand pies yet. Perhaps her sand isn't wet enough. Or perhaps she didn't pat it down properly.

6 There's a splendid castle! Can you see the bucket that the girl has used for making the towers?

7 Dad's interested in the newspaper. He doesn't like playing with sand, but I bet he could make a good castle. Do you like grown-ups to play with you, or not?

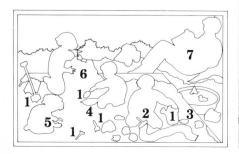

Talking Points

1 Do you think this sand is wet or dry or a bit of each? Who do you think is playing with dry sand? (Boy with sieve.) Whose sand must be a little wet? (Castle builder.)

2 How would you build a castle like that? What would you use to make flags? (Twigs, etc.) And other decorations? (Stones, shells.)

3 Do you think these children are sensibly dressed for playing in sand? They've still got their shoes and socks on – is that a good or a bad idea?

4 Do you think these children would like to build a castle together or do they like playing on their own? Would Dad like to share his paper with them? Would he prefer to be on his own?

Learning Skills

Sensations
Of course children know what sand feels like, but asking them to describe it encourages them to concentrate on particular sensations.
□ What does the sand going through the sieve feel like? (Dry, perhaps warm, quite soft.)
□ What about the castle builder's sand? (Damp, firm, quite hard.)
□ What does it feel like if you get it in your socks or pants? (Itchy, can get sore.)
□ What if you get it in your mouth? (Gritty.) Or eyes? (Very painful, which is why you must never throw it.)

Other people's feelings
When children play in this kind of situation they may become totally absorbed or they may try to interfere with others. They need to learn to respect other people's feelings.
□ Let's pretend that the little girl making sand pies gets bored and starts doing things that annoy the others.
□ What might she do to upset the boy with the rake? (Wipe out pattern.)
□ And the girl building the castle? (Knock it down.)
□ Would she be doing those things on purpose? (Yes.) What will the other children do to her if she does that to them? What might happen after that?
□ So what's Dad doing apart from reading? (Seeing there are no quarrels.)
Story and games on p.50

Toys

When given the opportunity to play with toy cars or other realistic models children can be very resourceful, using the toys to interpret situations they have come across in the real world.

☐ When playing with toy cars, children can build motorways, garages, bridges, tunnels – all the things they have seen on the roads.

☐ Old boxes, bricks, cardboard and models of houses or animals can all be brought in to make the game more exciting and to give children a chance to experiment.

☐ When children are playing side by side they often don't talk much or play together because they're so busy with their own toys.

Picture points

1 Let's look for all the things that roll on wheels. Have you noticed the car in the cushion garage?

2 The boy has made an interesting road, hasn't he? It goes up and down, over a bridge and through a tunnel. What kind of car is he pushing up the hill? What sort of noise do you think he is making? Can you make a car noise?

3 That truck's been given a hard push. How far do you think it will go?

4 The children are playing different games. Do you think they are happy playing by themselves? I expect they are sharing some of the toys.

5 Where have they used pieces of card, where an old box and where their building blocks? What have they used their dominoes for?

6 What other toys are the children using? (Animals, train, robot, etc.)

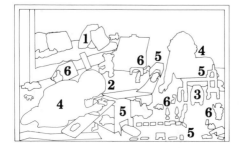

Talking Points

1 The boy is pushing the racing car up the slope. Have you ever been up a slope on your bike? Was it easy? Was it hard?

2 Will the boy have to push the car down the other side? Why not? What is biking downhill like? (Easier than up.)

3 What might happen when the racing car reaches the bottom? Will there be a crash? Then what will happen? (Front car will be pushed forwards.)

4 Do you think it would be easy to build roads like these? Would you like to try?

Learning Skills

Where things are

Young children need plenty of practice with words that indicate position. You can use several of the pictures in the set to do this kind of work.
☐ What's on the bed?
☐ What's just in front of it?
☐ What's in the toy box?
☐ What's under the book?
☐ Which toy is just behind the boy? (And so on.)
☐ What things are very near to the girl? What is a bit farther away? What is moving away from her?

Making things move

Many important principles are involved in making toys move. You can't teach these to young children, but your questions will make them aware of what is happening and so lay the foundations for later learning.
☐ What do cars have to help them move? (Wheels.) Is it easier to push a car that has wheels, or one that has lost them? What happens if it's only lost one wheel? Can it still go?
☐ Is it easier to push cars across a smooth floor or a rough carpet? Which would the car go farther on after just one push? Could you get it right across a carpeted room with one push?
☐ The children have made a ramp, or slope, for their cars. Do toy cars go up the ramp by themselves? Do they go down it by themselves?
☐ Can you think of anything else which would roll down that slope by itself? (Ball, cylinder, can, etc.) Would a building block roll down the slope? What about a domino?
Story and games on p.51

Playing With Puppets

Puppet play allows children to act out different roles: well-known fantasy roles such as Punch and Judy; adult roles such as a teacher or policeman; family roles where they can explore and express their feelings indirectly.

☐ You can put puppets on your hands and fingers and make them move almost like real people. You can pretend they are whoever you want them to be.

☐ Even if you're by yourself, you can put a puppet on each hand and let them have conversations with each other.

☐ Simple puppets are easily made from all kinds of things that you can find around the house.

Picture points

1 Snake is trying to sneak a drink, but it looks as though she may get a bang on the head from Dog. Do you think she'll get her drink or not?

2 The girl can get her hand right down the old sock so she can waggle Snake's head and tongue. The boy can get his fingers into Dog's paws.

3 There's another kind of puppet on a stick. As you twist the stick about the puppet moves its head and hands and its skirt sways around.

4 Have you seen the tiny mice on the girl's fingers? I wonder what she'll make them do? (Nibble little cakes, etc.)

5 The other girl is playing by herself and making her two puppets talk to each other.

6 Who's watching the puppet show? (Elephant, etc.) They're the audience.

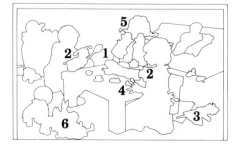

Talking Points

1 What do you suppose the girl is thinking? What she's going to make the puppet do next? (Lead towards the idea that although she's imagining she's the snake, she also has to stay outside the fantasy to work the puppet.)

2 What do you think the girl with the two puppets is thinking? (She has to remember both sides of the conversation she is making the puppets have.)

3 Is the little girl on the sofa using her teddy like a puppet? (No, but she's telling him a story, so he has a part to play even though she's not making him move like a puppet.)

4 Can any of the dolls and puppets really think? (No, but it's fun to pretend that they are like real people.)

Learning Skills

Colours
Children usually find it easiest to identify a familiar colour and show you where else that colour occurs before they go on to find another colour. Older children may progress to recognizing shades, but that is more difficult.
☐ Show me a red dress. Who else is wearing red?
☐ What colour are the teddy's foot and ear? Where can you see a nice bright red mouth? (Clown's face.) And bright red wheels? (On the blue toy truck.)
☐ Can you see anything that's a shade of red? (Elephant.) Do you know what colour that is? (Pink.) How is it made? (Mixing red and white together.)

What things are made of
It's always useful to point out exactly what things are made of, to discuss whether the materials are well chosen or not and to explain that many things can be made from discarded items.
☐ What is the snake made out of? (Old sock.)
☐ What about its tongue? (Felt.)
☐ And its eyes? (Buttons.)
☐ What else could you use to make a soft puppet like the snake? (Fur, any old clothes or pieces of fabric.)
☐ What could you use to make a stick puppet? (Old wooden spoon or dish mop.)
☐ What could you use to make finger puppets? (Old gloves.)
Story and games on p.52

IMAGINATIVE PLAY

Dressing Up

A dressing-up box is a valuable part of the toy cupboard, allowing children to act out their fantasies as they take on their own special versions of adult personalities.

☐ Dressing up is like getting into someone else's skin. You don't just put on their clothes, you can walk, talk and behave like them too.

☐ Sometimes we dress up as people we know – mums and dads, policemen, hairdressers – and sometimes we dress up as people we have seen on TV – astronauts, crooks, detectives, etc.

Picture points

1 There's a box full of dressing-up clothes. Most of the children have already dressed up, but there are plenty of things left if anyone wants to try on anything different. Look at the clothes that the children are wearing. Who has a headscarf? Dark glasses? A crown? A necklace? (Name each object.)

2 When the children have dressed up, they walk and talk like the person they are pretending to be. The clown has put on special make-up to help him look real, and the gangster and the smart lady are acting very well, aren't they?

3 Can you see children pretending to be someone they know well? (A mum and a dad.) Someone at work? (A hairdresser.) Someone in a book or on TV? (Superman.)

4 If you find a piece of flowing material you can pretend to be a dancing princess, or a river, or a butterfly.

5 Dressing up is much more fun if you can see what you look like. How many people are looking in a mirror? Who's saying "Hey, look at me"?

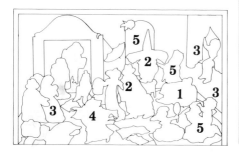

Talking Points

1 If you were with these children, would you like to dress up on your own like Superman or the princess, or would you rather dress up with a friend like the mum and dad or the gangster and the smart lady? Why?

2 Where do you think all these clothes came from? Who used to wear them? Why don't they wear them any more?

3 What would you choose to wear if you were one of the dressers? Which hat, coat, shoes? Would you put anything else on? What are your own favourite dressing-up clothes?

Learning Skills

Naming

Young children learn to recognize objects by working out the nature of their essential properties. They will soon be able to name a hat, whatever it looks like, because they know it is a piece of clothing that sits on top of the head.

☐ Show me all the children who are wearing hats.

☐ Point to any children who are not wearing hats.

☐ Is there a hat that no one is wearing yet? What colour is it?

☐ Is anyone wearing something on their head that isn't a hat? (Scarf, paper bag, crown, wig.)

☐ Can you draw me lots of different kinds of hats? (You are not looking for accurate drawings, but a recognition of different hat shapes.)

☐ Who do you know who wears a special hat? (Policeman, miner, traffic warden, nurse, etc.)

Real and pretend

It's worth asking older children to think about the difference between role play and the realities of the job.

☐ That girl is doing a hairdresser's job, isn't she? Does she look like a real hairdresser? Is she using the same things as a hairdresser?

☐ What are the differences between her and a real hairdresser?

☐ What about the girl having her hair done: does she feel that it's real or only pretend? She is having her hair done, but perhaps she won't keep it like that for long. Maybe just until bedtime. Could she go to school like that?

Story and games on p.53

IMAGINATIVE PLAY

Doctors And Nurses

When children dress up as people at work, they become aware of those people's jobs and of the thoughts and feelings that preoccupy them. Games of "Doctors and Nurses" help children to learn about caring for others and about working together to do so.

☐ Children often dress up and pretend to be different people.

☐ You don't need special outfits because you can find bits and pieces around the house to make uniforms and children often play more imaginatively in makeshift materials.

☐ Doctors and nurses look after people who are ill and make them better with instruments, bandages and medicine.

Picture points

1 These children are playing "Doctors and Nurses". They look very busy, just like real doctors and nurses.

2 Guess what happened to each of the toys. Is the boy really hurt or is he just pretending? What was he playing before he was a patient?

3 That teddy has a thermometer in its mouth. Thermometers tell the doctor if you have a temperature or not.

4 Those pieces of paper with lines on are charts to show if the patient's temperature is going up or down.

5 The nurse is wearing a face mask to stop germs getting from her to the patients. What could we use to make a mask and a nurse's uniform?

6 Apart from bandages and instruments, what else will make the patients feel better? (Fruit, hot water bottle.)

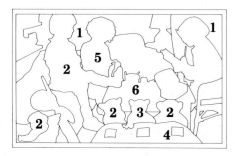

Talking Points

1 In the border are some of the things you would need to nurse someone. Do you know what they are all called?

2 Why does the nurse have her watch pinned to her apron? ("So she can see the time easily" is an acceptable answer. Not many children will know about pulse rates, but explain if they are interested. Can they feel yours?)

3 If the medicine was real, what do you think it would taste like? But it's pretend medicine. What could you use for that?

4 Who would you like to be: the doctor, the nurse, or the patient? Why?

Learning Skills

How to...
Children should be taught to recognize the need for basic first-aid as soon as they are old enough to understand its importance.
☐ How do you know that someone needs first-aid?
1 If they are bleeding
2 If they are lying still
3 If it hurts them to move
4 If their face is changing colour
5 If they are sick
☐ What would you do then?
(They should fetch an adult, NOT try to do something themselves.)
☐ What do you do before you bandage a cut? (Wash the cut, even if it looks clean. Cleanliness is the most important thing for all small cuts and grazes. See ABOUT OUR BODIES, p.42.)

Accident!
Teach children a simple procedure to follow if one of their friends has an accident out of sight of an adult.
☐ If you are playing and someone has an accident – perhaps cuts himself badly or is lying on the ground quite still – what do you do?
☐ One person stays with whoever is hurt. Others call or run for an adult. If there are only two of you, tell the hurt person that you are going for help and then run to find an adult. (Make sure children understand that a real accident is not the time for playing doctors. They will only make things worse. Real accidents need real doctors.)
Story and games on p.54

Pirates

Imaginative role-playing is an important part of children's personal development, teaching them observation, self-confidence and the value of friendly co-operation.

☐ Playing "Pirates" involves imaginary boats, desperate battles, walking the plank, secret strongholds and dressing up to look fierce.

☐ A few simple props are always helpful in these games, but children very quickly learn to invent imaginative uses for ordinary household objects.

☐ When children play together they often share and adapt each other's ideas as the game progresses.

Picture points

1 The children used an upside-down table for their ship. Can you think of anything else they could have used? (A box, chairs, chalked outline.)

2 What is that boy looking through? It's a pretend telescope. Telescopes help you to see things a long way away. What is he pretending to see? Who else has got something for looking through?

3 Some children have made pirate hats. Can you see what they are made from? Which pirates are wearing things from the kitchen? Do you think they make good helmets?

4 Which child is pretending to swim in the sea? Could you do that? Show me.

5 The pirate flag is supposed to frighten the enemy. What is on the flag? What else could you draw on it to make it frightening? Can you see another flag?

6 Is anyone in the boat not playing "Pirates"? Do you think he minds or is he happy playing by himself?

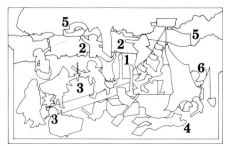

Talking Points

1 Which child do you think is the pirate captain? How can you tell?

2 Do you play pretend games with your friends? Who? What do you play? (Don't worry if your child has imaginary friends. This is not an indication of extreme loneliness, more a sign of an active imagination.)

3 What story do you think the children are acting? (People escaping from pirates, or small boats attacking pirates, pirate escaping, etc.)

Learning Skills

Real and pretend
Younger children can be encouraged to think how they could use ordinary objects for imaginary play. For older children, the dividing line between the real and imaginary worlds is a thin one, and you may need to keep an eye on their games if overexcitement and tears are to be avoided.

☐ What sort of things have the children used for the boats? Are they real boats? Are they good shapes for boats? See that little boat caught on that boy's fishing rod? What's it made of?

☐ How many of these boats would really float? (Most of them.) But would they be safe to use as boats on the water? (Cardboard boats would sink very fast, tin boats would tip over, table boats couldn't be controlled.)

☐ Are those real swords, or are they made so they won't hurt? Are those children really fighting? What should they be careful of? (Eyes.)

Role play
Children often need a few suggestions to help them decide how they will act out their roles. They can adapt your ideas as necessary.

☐ If you were the pirate captain, what would you tell your pirates to do? (Capture the escaping pirate, fight off the attacking small boats, etc.)

☐ If you were in a small boat, how would you organize an attack on the pirates? (Call to everyone to charge at once, surround the pirate ship and capture the captain.)

☐ What do you think will happen to the escaping pirate? Will she get away with the money? Will she be captured?
Story and games on p.55

EARLY RULES

Party Games

Games are the most exciting part of a children's party, but everyone needs to be made aware of the rules if the party-stopping cry "That's not fair!" is to be avoided.

☐ Blind Man's Buff involves all the elements – surprise, excitement, noise – which make up a good party game.

☐ In some party games there are winners and losers; in some games everyone is against everyone else; and in others there are teams. A few games don't have winners or losers at all – everyone plays just for fun.

☐ You have to get all the things you need for the games ready in advance so the party goes smoothly.

☐ It doesn't matter too much if you don't win. At least you've enjoyed playing the game.

Picture points

1 Here's a game of Blind Man's Buff in full swing. The Blind Man has just missed a boy. Is she going the right way to catch any of the others?

2 Can you see someone who'll be caught if she's not careful? How is she taking care not to get caught?

3 Two boys are keeping out of the game for a little while so they can share a joke, and some children would rather eat the party tea. Can you see someone who's had an accident?

4 How do we know that it's a party? (Balloons, streamers, hats, etc.)

5 The smallest person is playing her own game by herself. She looks happy.

6 What game did the children play before this one? You have to be blindfolded in that too, don't you?

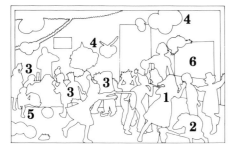

Talking Points

1 What do you think the children have had to eat and drink at this party? What do you like to eat at parties?

2 Everyone enjoys party games, but you have to know the rules to play them. What are the rules of Blind Man's Buff? If you were the Blind Man, what would you do to catch someone? How would you avoid being caught if you were one of the others?

3 What's your favourite party game? What are its rules? Why do you like it?

4 If you had a party, who would you invite? What would you have to eat? What games would you play?

Learning Skills

Sensations
Blind Man's Buff gives you a good chance to talk about the sense of touch.
□ When the Blind Man catches someone, how will she know who it is? (She'll have to feel them.)
□ How could you recognize someone by touching them? (Height, hair texture and length, features, clothes.)
□ Suppose she catches the girl in front of her, what will she find out? (She has short, curly hair; is wearing a dress; how tall she is, etc.)
□ Let's go round all the children playing and see how you could identify them. What do you think you would notice about your own friends?

Other people's feelings
Party games generate a good deal of excitement, but that excitement takes different forms. You might like to talk to your children about specific emotions; relate them to experiences you know they have enjoyed.
□ How do you know when people are happy? (Smiling faces, laughter.)
□ Who may be just about to get caught here? What does she feel like? (Excited, giggly, nervous.)
□ Does the Blind Man know she's there? How does she feel? (Much the same, perhaps a bit worried too.)
□ The boy with the striped T-shirt has made that girl spill her drink. How does he feel? (Sorry, or too excited to notice.) And what about her? (Cross.) Who will have to clear it up?
Story and games on p.56

Hide And Seek

Hiding games help to build a child's confidence and also to clarify the puzzling notion that something may be there even if it can't be seen.

☐ Hiding games are exciting for the people hiding and for the person looking.

☐ We have to learn to keep the rules or else the game will be spoilt.

☐ Hiding really well and not getting found is difficult. You have to keep very still and very quiet.

☐ It's no good leaving your head or your feet sticking out of your hiding place; you'll be found.

☐ Most animals are much better hiders and seekers than people are.

Picture points

1 How many people can you see hiding? Who has got the best place? Who has the worst place?

2 The flag marks the searcher's base. She has to try to find everyone before they creep up to the base.

3 Who do you think will be found by the searcher? And who probably won't be found unless the searcher looks very carefully?

4 The dog is about to find one of the hiders because it can smell him.

5 What do the two children under the big leaves feel like? Do you think they're excited? Do you think they'll stay hiding until they're found?

6 Can you see any animals hiding? If you were up in a tree or among the bushes, what other very small animals might you find? (Ladybirds, ants, woodlice, beetles, etc.)

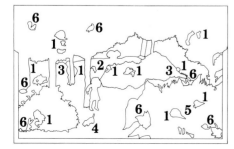

Talking Points

1 The searcher had to count up to twenty before she started looking for her friends. Do you think she counted for long enough or do you think she broke the rules? What do you do when you are playing?

2 What time of year do you think it is? How do you know? Do you think there are more hiding places in the summer than in the winter? Why?

3 Where do you think the dog would hide if it wasn't helping the searcher? Are all the animals well hidden? Some aren't hiding at all, are they?

4 If you were one of the people hiding, where would you go? Do you think you would be found or not?

5 If you wanted to hide at home, where would be the very best place?

Learning Skills

Position
This exercise provides practice with words denoting position. Confusion sometimes results when somebody moves and their position changes.
☐ Can you see someone peering out from behind the tree?
☐ Who's underneath the bush?
☐ That little girl is looking for people. Who is very near? Who is a long way away? Who is in front of her? Who is behind her? Who is above her?
☐ What will happen when she turns around? Who will be in front of her then? And who will be behind her?

How to hide
Although children will go off to hide or to seek quite happily, they find it difficult to do it systematically. This exercise will help them work out a successful plan.
☐ Who in the picture has not found a very good place to hide? Why? What will happen? Will they be easy to find?
☐ What do you have to do to hide? Does it matter if your feet stick out? Does it matter if you make a noise? Do you think it's a good idea to pop your head out to see what's going on? Why not?
☐ How would you catch everybody? (Wait by flag for people to pop heads out, or go and search the bushes and risk them creeping up to flag.)
Story and games on p.57

KEEPING RULES

Indoor Games

Board and card games are more difficult to understand than party games, and children enjoy them more when an adult joins in to help. This picture points out the difference between skill and luck.

☐ There are many different board and card games and each has its own set of rules, which we have to know before we can play properly.

☐ Although you need only good luck to win some games, in most of them you need a great deal of skill.

☐ Mums, dads and older brothers or sisters are often better at indoor games, but they can teach us how to play them and become good at them.

Picture points

1 Grandpa is helping the girls to play Snakes and Ladders. What do you think he's doing? (Helping to count spaces, making sure they play in turn.)

2 Do you already know how to play Snakes and Ladders, or would you need to read that book of rules? What will happen if one of the girls lands on a snake – or on a ladder?

3 Do you know what Grandma and the boy are playing? Why is he looking so worried? (Grandma's next move may "take" some more of his pieces.)

4 How do you play Dominoes? Is the little boy playing properly? No, but he's enjoying himself anyway, isn't he?

5 You need dice to play some games. Shake them out and you get numbers that help you win if you're lucky.

6 Grandpa is in the middle of a game of Patience. Can you play any card games?

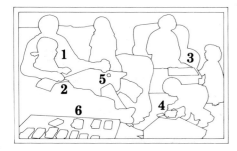

Talking Points

1 There are thousands of different games to play. When do you think people like to play these games? (During wet weather, before bedtime, on holiday, on long journeys, etc.)

2 Every game has its own rules. Let's think what would happen if people changed the rules: in Snakes and Ladders, what would happen if you could go up the snakes as well as the ladders?

3 Look at all the games in the picture. Which do you think need luck if you are going to win? Which need a lot of thought? Which do you think is the easiest to play? And which is the hardest? What about .... (eg Tiddly-winks)? Is it easy to play? (Encourage children to order the games, from the easiest to the most difficult.) Which do you need the most luck for?

Learning Skills

Shapes

As children learn to identify common shapes, they will also discover that each shape is appropriate for some purposes and not others.

☐ What shape are the dominoes? (Flat, long, quite thick.) That's why the boy can build with them. Could he build as easily with the cards or the draughts? (The cards are flat and long but they're also thin and bendy. The draughts are thick but also round and wobbly.)
☐ What shape is the dice? (Cube, ie six sides, all squares.) Would a round dice be any good? (Roll off board, couldn't be sure which number was showing.)

Luck and skill

Children often confuse "luck" and "skill". A few minutes' thought about this may help them to play complicated games more successfully.

☐ When you shake the dice, can you get the number you want just by thinking about it? Or by shaking the shaker in a special way?
☐ Wouldn't it be good if there was a magic word or a special way to shake the shaker to help you get the number you want? But it's just luck, isn't it?
☐ What about when you move the draughts? Is it luck where you move them? Is it bad luck when your piece gets taken?
Story and games on p.58

Outdoor Games

Playing games with other children is a major part of a child's social life. To do this successfully she must know how a game is played and be prepared to stick to the rules.

☐ Games like hopscotch, marbles or chasing games are for children. You don't need a special place to play them; they are fun to play anywhere.

☐ Children's games have rules just as adults' games do. You have to know how to play if everyone is going to enjoy themselves.

☐ Some games, like football, have rules made up by adults; some are learned from songs or rhymes; and some are made up by children.

Picture points

1 How many balls can you see? What are the children doing with the balls? Can you see the basketball players? What do they have to do? Do grown-ups play basketball?

2 Do you know what those little round things are? What are they made of? How do you play marbles?

3 Do you know how to play hopscotch? What do you use to throw into the squares? Do grown-ups usually play?

4 Those children are playing tag. Who is chasing? Who is going to be caught? What will happen after she's caught? (She will become the chaser.)

5 The goalkeeper is waiting for the others to kick the ball at the goal. He will try to stop it going in.

6 Do you know any skipping songs that these children might be singing?

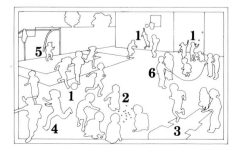

Talking Points

1 The little girl wearing a sling is talking to a friend. What will happen if she stops turning the rope? (It will spoil the game for everyone.)

2 Could the children playing marbles use stones instead? Why not? (You may have to explain the game before asking this question.)

3 Could the children throwing balls against the wall use stones? (Stones are dangerous and they don't bounce very well.)

4 Which games do not need balls or stones or marbles or ropes? (Two games: tag and hoop rolling.)

Learning Skills

Actions
There is plenty of activity in this picture. Adapt ideas from other pictures to start discussions about colour, shape, numbers, etc. Here are some ideas for sorting out vocabulary connected with movement.

☐ How are all these children moving? Who's hopping?

☐ Who else is playing a game with lots of hopping, skipping and jumping? (Skipping game.)

☐ Who is doing what in the skipping game? (Two are turning the rope, one is skipping, two waiting their turn, one watching sadly.)

☐ Who's kicking? Who's bouncing a ball? Who's running?

Other people's feelings
Most children understand what it feels like to be shy, lonely, impatient, etc, but may be unable to express themselves. It is reassuring for them to know that these feelings are universal, so talk them through such situations.

☐ Look at the boy standing by himself. How is he feeling? Why isn't he joining in the skipping game? Would you ask him to join in?

☐ Some of the children are waiting and watching. Why do you have to wait for a turn? Do you ever find it difficult to wait? What would happen if everyone tried to skip at once?

☐ Someone else is playing by himself too. (Hoop roller.) Do you think he is lonely or not?

Story and games on p.59

KEEPING RULES

Football

As children begin to participate in team games, they discover the sometimes uncomfortable fact that rules are essential to the game's success and cannot be broken without consequences.

☐ Footballers play in two sides of eleven players each. If anyone breaks the rules, the other side gets an advantage.

☐ The referee makes sure everyone plays to the rules and blows the whistle to tell the players when to stop or start.

☐ Each side tries to score goals by kicking the ball into the other team's goal. The side with most goals at the end of the game is the winner.

Picture points

1 The two teams are wearing different coloured shorts and shirts. Why? They have numbers on their shirts to show their position on the field.

2 Who has just kicked the ball? Who did he kick it to? Where will that boy try to kick it next? (Goal.) Can you point to all the other players on that side?

3 There are many different rules to this game. One is that the team have to play only inside the football pitch. Can you see the edges of the pitch? Can you see where the goal-line is? It's only a goal if the ball goes completely over the line.

4 The referee has had to blow her whistle because one boy has pushed another boy over. That's a foul. The other side will be given a free kick.

5 There's the goalkeeper. His job is to stop the ball getting into the goal.

6 All the players are wearing football boots. What does the underneath of their boots look like? (Studded.) Why?

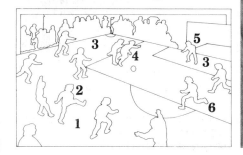

Talking Points

1 The referee is busy watching what is happening in the game. I wonder what would happen if she wasn't there. Could you have a match without the referee? (Almost impossible!)

2 Look at the people watching the game. They are supporting the different teams. Who is supporting the reds?

3 Do you have a football team you support? Which one? Would you like to go and watch them when they are playing at home? What do the supporters do when their team scores? When the other team scores? When the other team gets a free kick? Do they think it's fair? Are they being fair?

Learning Skills

Rules

Rather than attempting to explain the rules of such a complicated game, concentrate on those principles that would apply to most team games.

☐ The players try to kick the ball into the goal. How else could they get it in? (By heading it.) Could they throw it in? Why can't they use their hands? (It's against the rules – this is *foot*ball.)

☐ Why mustn't they kick each other? (Against rules and dangerous.)

☐ Why mustn't the referee support one side and not the other? (Not fair.)

Other people's feelings

Children who have played a team game or who are eager spectators will be able to understand the picture better and talk to you about their feelings.

☐ What do you think the people watching feel like? Are they excited, nervous, worried, angry? (It depends which team they're supporting.)

☐ Are the players excited too or are they too busy thinking about all the things they've got to do?

☐ What will the boy who is being knocked over be thinking? What about the goalkeeper? What about the referee? (Answers will vary depending on how much your child already knows about football.)

☐ Can you see the two players waiting on the side of the pitch? They are the reserves. How are they feeling? (Supporting their side and also hoping to get a chance to play.)

Story and games on p.60

Making Music

Playing music well requires practice, application and often a willingness to co-operate with others. This picture will also enable children to discuss how different musical sounds are made.

☐ Making music is fun but it is also hard work and difficult to do.

☐ Children often play instruments together in school. Everyone plays their own music and the sounds mix.

☐ The many different instruments form a small number of main groups. Some boom, some bang, some whistle, some tinkle like bells.

☐ If you want to play well you have to practise and learn to play the notes loudly, softly, quickly and slowly.

Picture points

1 These children are having a music lesson. Can you see the teacher?

2 There is one girl playing the drum. She is playing the beat (explain "beat" if necessary) to keep everyone in time.

3 The teacher is being the conductor. He shows the players when to stop and start and helps them play together.

4 Look at all the different instruments. (Point to each one and name it.) What sort of sound do you think this one makes? (Go through, eg xylophone with wooden keys, glockenspiel with metal keys, recorders, drum, tambourine.)

5 Those children are playing recorders. Can you see how they fit their fingers over the holes to change the notes?

6 Can you see any other instruments in the picture? (Guitar, piano.)

7 I can see something else that makes music as well. (Record player.)

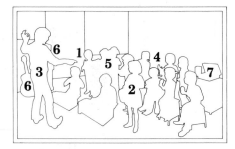

Talking Points

1 When you play an instrument you have to learn the right way to use your hands. Tell me how all the players are using theirs. Which other part of your body do you use to play other instruments? (Mouth, lips.)

2 You also have to learn not to bang or blow too loudly. Who would make much too much noise if they banged too hard?

3 Which children are not playing at the moment? Do you think they are waiting to play when it's their turn? Do you think they have forgotten when to play?

4 When you first start playing an instrument it often doesn't sound very nice. Would you enjoy practising hard so that you could play well?

Learning Skills

Same and different
Musical instruments tend to come in families, often differing from each other only slightly. As a rule small members of each family are pitched high and the larger ones pitched low.
□ Show me all the children who have instruments to blow. Are they all the same? (No, some smaller, some bigger.)
□ Which two instruments do you shake to make a noise? (Shakers, tambourine.) Are they the same?
□ Which instruments do we hit to make a noise? (Drums, tambourine, xylophone, triangle.)
□ Those two instruments are played in the same way but they are not the same. (Xylophone has wooden keys, glockenspiel has metal keys.)

Sounds
Distinguishing the sounds made by different instruments is useful for more advanced musical appreciation later.
□ What makes a banging sort of noise? (Drums, tambourine.)
□ What sort of noise does a recorder make? (It whistles like a bird.)
□ Which instrument makes a sound like bells? (Triangle.)
□ Which instruments in the picture can only play one note? (Drum, shakers.) Which can play lots of different notes, some high and some low? (Piano, guitar, recorders, xylophone, glockenspiel.)
Story and games on p.61

The Band

A band is a good example of co-operative effort in action. Learning to work with others is an important part of growing up. Although children soon learn that it can be a frustrating business, they can also begin to discover its rewards.

☐ When we have learned to play a musical instrument we can start to play tunes with other people.

☐ Playing in a band is one of the things adults and children can do successfully together.

☐ Different instruments make different sounds. Together these make one big tune which everyone can hear.

☐ The band leader shows people how fast to play and when to come in, so everyone has to watch him carefully.

Picture points

1 People in a band often wear the same sort of clothes. Some look very smart, but I can see some players who haven't got hats. Can you find them?

2 The band is marching through the town. The leader waves his stick to help the players keep in time.

3 Look how the books of music are fixed on to the instruments. The book tells the players what tune to play.

4 Not all the instruments are played together all the time. Sometimes the drum is played by itself to help the band keep in step as they march.

5 Can you see some people in the band who look as if they are enjoying themselves? And someone who's had an accident? What has happened?

6 Some spectators are marching along with the band. Are they in the way? What do you think the dogs might do?

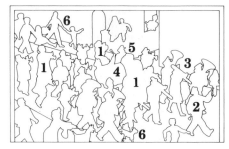

Talking Points

1 How many different instruments can you count in the picture? Which is the biggest? Which one would you most like to play?

2 This is called a brass band, where all the instruments except the drum are made of metal and you have to blow through them to make them sound. Do you know what all the blowing instruments are called? (Cornet, trumpet, trombone, euphonium, tuba, French horn.)

3 Can you think of any instruments you know which aren't in the picture? You couldn't walk along playing a piano or an organ, could you?

4 What would happen if there wasn't a leader? What if someone had the music for a different tune to everyone else?

Learning Skills

What people are doing
Younger children will probably find the spectacle of a real band too exciting to concentrate on how any particular instrument is being played, so help them by going through the picture.
☐ How is the drummer making a sound with his instrument?
☐ What are the other players doing to make sounds with their instruments? (Blowing.)
☐ Apart from blowing, most of the players have to do something else to make different notes. Do you know what that is? (Press down knobs – valves.)
☐ Which of these blowing instruments does not have valves? (Trombone.) How do the trombone players make different notes? (Move slide up and down.)

Sounds
Do as much as you can to help children recognize different sounds and apply those sounds to specific instruments. The Study Box on p.62 will help with this exercise.
☐ All these blowing instruments make different sounds. Which ones make big, deep sounds?
☐ Which make high, shriller sounds?
☐ Which instrument makes very loud booms to help everyone keep in time?
☐ Let's make all those sounds.
Story and games on p.62

Disco Dancing

Disco dancing permits a wide range of movement, and consequently offers an opportunity for children to express themselves freely by developing their own individual dancing style.

☐ Discos are fun! They are called discos because the music comes from discs (or records). The DJ puts them on the turntable and plays them loudly through the amplifier and speakers.

☐ The lights are all different colours and they flash on and off as the music plays. It's quite dark most of the time.

☐ You can dance with your friends, just one person, or by yourself. You just do whatever you feel like doing.

☐ Some people dress up very smartly and others don't bother. You can usually wear whatever you like.

Picture points

1 When people dance, they move different parts of their bodies. Can you see people moving their arms and legs in different ways?

2 These five dancers are all kicking their legs to the music. It's difficult for them to keep in time with each other.

3 Those people near the speaker are trying to talk to each other. I bet they can't hear anything except the music!

4 Who came in their ordinary clothes and who put on something special?

5 There are drinks for people who are hot and thirsty. What drink would you choose if you'd been dancing?

6 The DJ talks into his microphone to say what the next record is and who chose it.

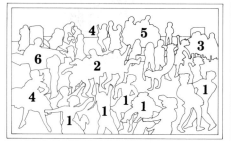

Talking Points

1 Which clothes do you like best? Which of your own clothes would you wear to a disco? Why would you choose them?

2 Have you seen people dancing like this on television? Which programme were they on? What is your favourite song at the moment? Can you sing it? Can you dance to it?

3 The loud music makes it easy to dance because you can hear the beat. If the music is very loud, what can it stop you from doing? (Talking, thinking.)

4 We still have dances with special names where the music tells you how you must move. It's not always easy and you have to learn the steps and practise them. Do you know the names of any of these dances? (Waltz, etc.)

Learning Skills

Numbers
The picture gives you a chance to practise some of the words that are a useful part of early number work.
☐ Can you show me the people dancing by themselves? They're all alone, aren't they? Do you know a word for one person or thing by itself? (Single.)
☐ What about the sets of two people dancing together, do you know a name for two together? (Pair.)
☐ How many pairs and how many single people can you spot? Are there more single people or more pairs? One of the reasons why disco dancing is fun is because it doesn't matter whether you dance singly or in a pair. You can do whatever you like.

Other people's feelings
Perhaps understandably, younger children find teenage emotions the object of enormous hilarity, but they can also learn to treat them sensibly.
☐ Can you see the two people alone and not dancing? What's the boy thinking, do you think? And the girl? Should they ask each other to dance?
☐ Suppose one wanted to dance and the other didn't. Could they say "no" without upsetting each other?
☐ There are two people kissing each other and two girls laughing at them. What do you think – is kissing funny, or fun, or serious?
Story and games on p.63

PHYSICAL SKILLS

Swimming

It is vitally important that children should learn to swim, for their own safety. Later, they can go on to master the wide variety of skills involved in being a good swimmer and diver.

☐ Swimming is fun and it's useful: if you fall into water you know what to do.

☐ It's best to learn to swim in a pool where the water is warm and shallow and there are plenty of people to help.

☐ Once you've learned to swim, you can work out all the different strokes and learn to dive.

Picture points

1 Everyone's at the swimming pool. Who is this side of the rope? (Children learning to swim and parents.)

2 Show me all the things for helping learners to keep afloat. You can't sink in the water if you're using them.

3 This boy is just putting on his arm bands. What is his big sister blowing into them? (Air.)

4 Which people in the big pool are swimming on their fronts? Which on their backs? Who is having fun just splashing about? Who is floating?

5 That boy is going to dive. He'll go right in, head first. Would you like to do that? Do you mind putting your face under the water?

6 The attendant is blowing his whistle to tell those boys to stop jumping off the side. Why is jumping in dangerous? (Might land on someone else.)

7 That baby is holding out her arms for her dad to take her into the water. Do you think she's frightened? Will her dad let her go when she's in the water?

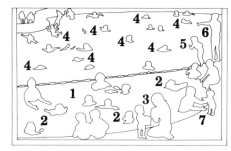

Talking Points

1 How deep do you think the water is in the learners' part? Could you stand up in it? (Yes.) Is it deeper in the other part of the pool?

2 In the learners' part, which children look as if they can nearly swim? Who is only just starting to learn?

3 Do you know what all the strokes are called? (Breaststroke, crawl, backstroke, butterfly.) Can you show me how to do them? Is anyone in the big pool doing them?

4 Why do you have to dry yourself straight after swimming and not sit around when you're still wet? (May catch a chill.)

Learning Skills

Where things are
This is a good picture for practising words that describe position. Remember that we use these words in all sorts of different situations and so your child will take some time to learn to use them in all the ways we do.
☐ Who is in the water? Who is out of the water? Who is going into the water?
☐ Who is half in and half out of the water? Which half is wet? Which is dry?
☐ Whose face is under water? (You could point out that most of the people swimming properly are doing this.) Whose head is out of the water?
☐ Who's got arm bands on to help them float and keep their heads and arms out of the water?

How to visit the swimming pool
Most leisure activities involve similar procedures. It's worth talking through these before you go out so that your child becomes familiar with the routine.
☐ When we go to the pool, what do we do first? (Pay to get in.)
☐ After we've paid, what do we do? Do we all use the same changing room?
☐ What do we do in the changing room? (Change, put clothes in locker, give key and valuables to attendant.)
☐ Then we can get straight in, can't we? (No, usually a footbath first.)
☐ How long do we swim for? (Until tired or cold, or until told to get out by parent or attendant.)
Then reverse procedures for going home. Story and games on p.64

PHYSICAL SKILLS

Ice Skating

Pages 18 *and* 38 *in* LEGS, WHEELS AND WINGS *concentrate on our ability to move quickly over ice and snow. This picture demonstrates that skating is both fun and highly skilful.*

☐ Ice is frozen water. It gets harder as the weather gets colder and then people can stand, skate and fall on it.

☐ Skates are long, thin, metal blades which cut through the top of the ice.

☐ Some people only ever learn to skate forwards, but others can dance, go backwards and stop suddenly.

☐ We have to practise hard if we are going to be good at sports such as skating and swimming.

Picture points

1 Such a lot of people have come skating today! Show me those who are really good at it.

2 Some of the learners don't yet feel safe enough to set out by themselves. Can you see someone who is hanging on to an adult? There's a boy who is pushing a chair along to help keep himself up. Is there anyone else who looks as though they are trying to skate for the first time? How do you think they feel?

3 Show me the person who has slipped on the ice and fallen over. He really seems to be enjoying himself. It's very easy to fall over on the ice because it's so slippery.

4 Some people have joined together to make a long chain. Why will they have to take great care? (Not to pull each other over or knock anyone down.)

5 Look at the patterns made by the blades of the skates cutting into the ice. We can see exactly where the skaters have been.

Talking Points

1 Why do you think some people in the picture can skate so much better than others? (Practise, teaching.)

2 Can you think of any sorts of skates that don't need ice? (Roller skates.)

3 What other ways are there of going fast over ice and snow? (Skis, toboggans. See LEGS, WHEELS AND WINGS.)

4 What's the difference between skating in an ice-rink and on a river or pond? (You have to make sure that the ice is thick enough to hold you. Ask Mum or Dad before you go on a frozen pond, whether walking or skating.)

Learning Skills

Numbers: grouping
The people are placed so as to allow you to pick out small groups with your child. Young children may see the pair in front easily, but they will not necessarily spot all the other pairs immediately. Take it slowly.
☐ Let's see who is on their own and who has come with friends.
☐ How many people are by themselves?
☐ How many groups of two people can you see? Show them all to me.
☐ Can you see two groups of three people?
☐ Can you see a larger group of people all together? (The chain.) Do you know how many people there are in the chain? Let's count them.

What ice is like
Ask your child to think of the best words to describe a piece of ice. Then talk about each word in a way that will help her understand the nature of ice more fully.
☐ Ice is cold – hard – light – smooth.
☐ What else is cold? (Snow, wind, sea-water, ice-cream, etc.)
☐ What else is hard? (Stones, wooden table.) Show me some hard things.
☐ What else is light? (Feathers, paper.)
☐ What else is smooth? (Apple, glass.)
Older children may produce answers that use two or more of these descriptions. Encourage your child to think about such combinations:
☐ What else is cold and hard? Cold and light? Cold and smooth? Hard and light? Hard and smooth? Light and smooth?
Story and games on p.65

PHYSICAL SKILLS

Fishing

Fishing is not only a popular pastime, it has the added attraction of occasionally providing a well-earned meal for the lucky angler.

☐ Fish live in water. Some live in fresh water – rivers, streams, lakes, ponds – and others live in the sea, where the water is salty.

☐ Fish is a food that is tasty and very good for our bodies.

☐ Men and women all over the world earn a living by selling the fish they catch. (See THE FOOD WE EAT, p.20.)

☐ Lots of people spend their free time trying to catch fish. Sometimes they eat the fish they catch, but often they just put them back in the water.

Picture points

1 People who go fishing for fun with rods and lines are called anglers. Grown-ups and children can be anglers. Can you see what all the children in this picture are doing?

2 These anglers are fishing from a pier. They can let their lines down into deep water where the fish are without having to go out in a boat.

3 You don't have to use a rod and line to catch fish. Can you see someone who's using a handline?

4 Who has caught some fish? Who is just catching a fish? Who have caught enough fish and are going home? Who has caught something that isn't a fish? Could he eat it all the same?

5 All the anglers have some bait with them. What are all the other things they use called? (Rod, line, reel, etc.)

6 Do you know what a lifebelt is for? Show me one in the picture.

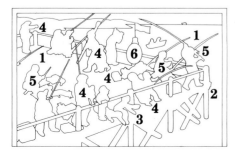

Talking Points

1 Why have the two people chosen to go out in the boat to fish? (Better chance of catching fish, fewer people, different kinds of fish.)

2 Those two girls are pulling in a fish by winding a reel on their rod. What do you think that does? (Winds up the line and brings the fish with it.) Then the rod starts bending and the line gets tight.

3 How do anglers know when they've got a bite? (Feel a tug as the fish eats the bait.)

4 How do you feel about fishing? Do you think the anglers should put the fish back after they've caught them? Do you think the fish get hurt?

Learning Skills

What people are doing
It's always helpful for young children to be led into a picture by identifying individual actions.
☐ Who's holding a fishing rod?
☐ Who's sitting down?
☐ Who's caught some fish and is having a little sleep?
☐ Who's eating their lunch?
☐ Who's just putting his rod together?
☐ Who's going to cast his bait far out into the sea?
☐ Who is not fishing at all?

What things are for
Although children easily understand that anglers are trying to catch fish, they need to concentrate on individual ideas to work out how they do it.
☐ Let's talk about what they're going to use to catch fish. What do they have that the fish want to eat? (Bait.)
☐ Then they put on a sharp hook so that when the fish bites the bait it gets stuck on the hook. Can you see a hook? What is the hook fastened to so that the fish can be pulled out of the water? (Line and rod.)
☐ What sometimes happens to the lines? (They get tangled up.) Do you think that might happen here?
☐ These people are a long way from the fish in the water so they have to use long lines: what other way could they catch fish if they were closer to the water? (Shrimping nets. See ANIMALS OF OUR WORLD, p.14.)
Story and games on p.66

PHYSICAL SKILLS

A Ballet

Most children thoroughly enjoy moving to music and find it an exciting way to express emotions. You can help develop their skills even if you are quite sure you have no dancing talent yourself.

☐ You can dance just because you like moving your body to the music, but you can also dance to tell a story without using words.

☐ Ballet dancers usually dance on the stage in theatres.

☐ This ballet is called "Swan Lake". The dancers have to move so the audience knows they are pretending to be swans.

☐ Ballet dancers have to practise for many years to learn the movements and make their bodies strong.

Picture points

1 "Swan Lake" is about a prince who falls in love with the queen of the swans. She was turned into a swan by a wicked magician. Can you see the prince and the queen of the swans?

2 The dancers' dresses are all fluffed up to look like swans' feathers. They use their arms to imitate how swans move.

3 Have you seen who is about to enter the stage? The wicked magician is very angry with the prince.

4 There is the magician's enchanted castle. Is it a real castle?

5 The orchestra is playing the music for "Swan Lake" and the conductor has to make sure each musician plays his instrument at the right time. The timing is important for the dancers.

6 A male ballet dancer has to be strong as well as graceful in case he has to lift a female dancer right up in the air.

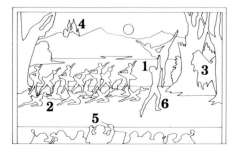

Talking Points

1 Have you ever seen a swan? (If "yes", what sort of movements could dancers make to look like swans?) The border shows how swans fly.

2 Which dancer in the picture is making the very best swan shape? Why did you choose that one?

3 At the end of the story of "Swan Lake" the swan queen and the prince die. What sort of music do you think goes with that bit of the story? (Sad, slow.)

4 Have you ever seen a ballet in a theatre or on television? Can you remember anything about it?

Learning Skills

Movement
It is not too difficult to help young children move rhythmically. If you lay the foundations, teachers and others can build on them later. Do the movements with them, starting with small movements and working up to more complicated manoeuvres.
□ Let's move our fingers in time.
□ Can you move your hand in time?
□ Can you move your arm and hand and finger in time? Both arms? The top half of your body? And your feet? (You may need to hold a younger child's hands. By this time you should be dancing together! You may have to remind young children to keep moving the various parts of their bodies.)

Real and pretend
Although it's always useful to point out the difference between real and imaginary worlds, it's also worth remembering that children still have an ability to immerse themselves in a story that most adults tend to lose. Make sure they know that you think emotional responses to such stories are very worthwhile.
□ Are the swans real swans? Is the prince really a prince? (And so on.)
□ Do the actors really die at the end of the story? Do the swans die?
□ If you know that the actors are only acting, why do you feel sad when the swans die? Is it because it's such a good story that you almost do believe it?
□ Would you want to watch the ballet if you knew you would feel sad at the end, or is it good to feel sad sometimes?
Story and games on p.67

PHYSICAL SKILLS

Hitting The Target

It takes more than a little luck to win a prize at a fair. This picture provides a good opportunity to discuss with children the disappointing fact that there are some skills that they may not master until they are older.

☐ Some games are just fun to play for themselves.

☐ Sometimes we like to see just how clever we are. At the fairground we can win prizes if we're good enough.

☐ You choose the stall where you want to try, and then pay the stallholder.

☐ If you win you get a prize, but even if you don't, it's still good fun.

Picture points

1 At the rifle range you try to shoot the toy ducks which are moving round. When you hit the duck it falls down and you may win a prize. Can you see what the prizes are?

2 At the hoop-la stall you have to throw a ring and get it right over one of the things on the stall. Has anyone won a prize? How could you win a prize on the coconut shy?

3 That boy and girl are counting their money to see if they have enough to have one more go.

4 On the slot machines you do not win prizes, but the better you are the more time you have on the machine. You put your money in and press a button. Lots of lights flash and things whizz about on a screen. These machines often test how fast you are.

5 Can you see people who've won prizes? Which stalls did they win them at? What did they have to do?

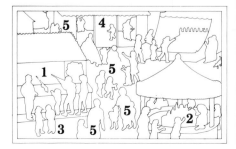

Talking Points

1 Look at the prizes to win on the stalls. Which one would you like? Which one would be easiest to win?

2 I wonder if that boy and girl saved their pocket money to go to the fair. Perhaps they want to win something special to give to their parents. Do you think so?

3 If we worked at a fair, which sort of stall would we own? Would you like to be the person in charge? Why?

4 Suppose you had gone to a fair and hadn't won anything – how would you feel? Would it have been worth going?

Learning Skills

Big and small
Children may be unwilling to admit that they have physical limitations, but talking about other people's capabilities should help them think about their own.
☐ Can you see someone who is too small to use a rifle at the rifle range? He will have to wait until he's older, won't he? What could he do instead?
☐ Look at the children at the hoop-la stall. Would they be big enough to have a go at shooting or not? (Probably not.)
☐ Can you see the baby beside the coconut shy? Could the baby hit a coconut? Is there anything at the fair that the baby could do? (Watch, eat!)

How to win a prize
Now concentrate on one particular stall and see if your child can work out all the actions involved. Relate the questions to his capabilities and arrange for some practice if you can.
☐ How do you have a go at the coconut shy? Tell me what you have to do first. (Pay for the balls.) And then? (Look at the coconuts to decide which one to throw at. Are any wobbly already?) And then? (Take aim.) How do you aim? (Watch what you want to hit very hard.) And then? (Throw straight.)
☐ Could you throw softly, or would you have to throw hard to knock a coconut off and win it?
☐ Do you think the coconut shy would be too difficult for you? Would you rather try something else, or do you think trying something hard would be fun even if you didn't win?
Story and games on p.68

PHYSICAL SKILLS

Tennis

Whether or not your child ever reaches competition standard in any sport, you can go with her to see tournaments and take the opportunity to explain rules and the importance of applying them fairly.

☐ You play tennis with a racket and ball. You have to try to hit the ball over the net and keep it inside the white lines. If you don't, the other side wins a point. You can play singles or doubles.

☐ In special matches there is an umpire, with judges to help him. They watch where the ball goes and make sure the players play fairly.

☐ All the spectators get very excited about who is winning or losing.

Picture points

1 Can you see the players? The ones on this side of the net are playing against the two on the other side of the net.

2 The players have to use their rackets to hit the ball over the net and inside the outer white lines.

3 When someone wins a point with a good shot, everyone watching will clap and cheer.

4 Who's got the best view? The umpire sits high up so he can see that everything is fair. He calls out the score after every point.

5 The umpire can't see everything because the ball goes very fast, so the judges help him. They each watch one of the lines to see whether the ball lands "in" or "out".

6 Ballboys help the players by picking up the balls when they land outside the court or hit the net. The players lose a point if they hit the ball into the net or outside the court.

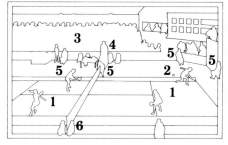

Talking Points

1 Near the umpire there are some empty chairs, some bottles, beakers and towels. What do you think those might be for? (The players rest and drink and wash quite often during the game.)

2 This is such an important match that it's being filmed for TV. Can you see the TV cameras? Which do you think is more exciting: going to the game, or watching it on TV?

3 What's that (scoreboard) for? (It tells everyone who is winning and losing.) In the first part of the match one side got six games and one got three. Who won?

Learning Skills

Positions and distances

Play a sort of guessing game to practise talking about positions and distances. Take it in turns to describe where something is and to identify the something from the description.

☐ I'm thinking of something: it's underneath the player's foot, on top of it and all round it – what is it? (Shoe and sock.)

☐ What is all around the court: down the sides, at the end and down the middle? (White lines.)

☐ What is in the air now but will hit the ground soon? (The ball.) Who hit the ball last? If she had hit it a little lower what would have happened? And if she had hit it a little harder?

☐ Who is going to hit the ball next? Where will he try to hit it? (Younger children may say "back, so that another player can have a turn to hit".)

Causes and consequences

This picture gives you a chance to do a bit of simple scientific experimenting. Try hitting a soft ball (of crumpled-up paper, perhaps) with a stick and talk about what happens.

☐ Let's see what we can do to make this paper ball move. Let's think of as many ways as possible. (Blowing, pushing, hitting...)

☐ If we hit it very slowly will it move a long way or a little way? Let's try.

☐ What do you think it will do if we hit it very fast?

☐ Where do we have to hit it if we want it to go up in the air? Sideways? Etc.

☐ Let's see if we can hit it into the wastepaper basket to tidy up!

Story and games on p.69

PHYSICAL SKILLS

At The Circus

Behind the glamour and excitement of the circus lies the reality of hard practice and an unstable nomadic life. Children find it difficult to realize that many of the tricks they see performed require a high degree of skill.

☐ Circuses are usually in very large, round tents called Big Tops.

☐ The people and animals perform in a ring inside the tent.

☐ Circus people have to practise hard. Some of them are very skilful at using their bodies, some train animals and some, like clowns, can do most things.

Picture points

1 Clowns like these can do all sorts of tricks which make us laugh.

2 One clown is flying through the air. The clown in the checked trousers has thrown him off his shoulders and he should land on the shoulders of the big clown. But what else might happen?

3 How many clubs is that clown juggling with? Why is he dropping them? Did he mean to?

4 The tallest clown is on stilts. He is carrying a very strange gun. Have you ever seen one like that? Would it make you laugh?

5 One clown is much shorter than the others. He is not a child; he is a midget. (Your child may not know that midgets exist and that they are ordinary people.)

6 Do you think that clown will get to the end of the tightrope without falling off? Why not?

7 Do you know a dog that could walk on a ball like this one? Why not? (This one has been carefully trained.)

Talking Points

1 The clowns are doing their act in the circus ring. Why is it called a ring? Why is it a good idea to do a show in a round space? (Wherever you sit you can see what is going on.)

2 Tell me what you think the people watching are thinking.

3 The circus moves from town to town, never stopping for long. What sort of homes do you think the circus people have? (Caravans.) Would you like to live in a caravan and travel about?

4 How do you think the animals get from one town to another? (Horse boxes and special cages.)

Learning Skills

Balancing
To see if your child understands the meaning of balancing, go through the balancing acts being performed here.
☐ There's a lot of balancing going on in the picture. Show me someone balancing on something narrow. Why is walking along a rope difficult?
☐ The dog is balancing on the ball. Why is that difficult?
☐ One clown is balancing on his stilts. Could you do that?
☐ Why is the seesaw down on one side and up on the other? How could you make the seesaw balance so that it was level? (Putting same weight on both ends, or no weight at all. Demonstrate, if necessary, with a ruler.)

Throwing and catching
Keep encouraging your child to practise skills he finds physically difficult. When he has mastered one he will feel more confident to tackle the next.
☐ Hold a ball in one hand. Throw it into the air and catch it in two hands. Then try catching it in one hand. Watch the ball all the time and then you won't drop it so often.
☐ Try throwing the ball from one hand to the other. Then pass the ball from the catching hand to the throwing hand and try again. Keep practising until you can do this quickly.
☐ Then you can try using two balls. This is difficult because you have to move two balls at the same time so you always have to have one ball in the air.
Story and games on p.70

— Checking Progress —

Is your child learning?

You can't test how well your child is doing in this kind of work because it is impossible to make a test that has any real value and, in any case, the whole process of deliberately testing a young child is more than likely to put him off working with you at all. However, if the work is going well, he will be acquiring and beginning to use new vocabulary, mastering all kinds of thinking skills, greatly increasing his manual and physical dexterity and be giving evidence of this in everything he does. Of course this only happens very gradually and you will probably want to pause now and then to see how things are going.

Keeping a record

The best way to record progress is to choose two or three of the pictures that seem to be your child's favourites and keep notes of what he does and says each time he looks at those pictures. You may not come back to them very frequently and so you may well find that you had not realized just how much more he has thought out from one session with a picture to the next. If you are really interested in your child's development you could add photographs of the models he makes or the games he plays to produce a small, very personal scrapbook. No doubt your child will enjoy helping you to keep it up to date.

Things to watch for

Concentration How long did your child concentrate on a picture? What sort of things distract him? What helps him to concentrate? Small children can quite easily be distracted by things going on around them, particularly when they're not sure what it is they are supposed to be doing. They'll show more interest and concentrate better if they understand the aim of the activity, can cope with its demands, and are receiving your support and praise when they try hard and do well. It's also important to concentrate yourself so that they can use you as a model for learning how to set about things.

Success Children, like the rest of us, enjoy success and dislike failing. They can also tell the difference between deserved praise and being fobbed off with "Oh, that's nice dear." So learning is most enjoyable when questions and problems can be dealt with successfully with a little bit of effort, and when they offer an opportunity to show off cleverness to an admiring public. This means you need to

organize your questions so that there are some the child can answer straight off, some that he can do with a little help from you, and none, or almost none, that he can't begin to manage. You know a lot about your child, which is the first step, and you can note what makes questions easier or harder for him. If he's being right all the time very easily you may like to try a few harder ideas – questions beginning "how" and "why" are usually more difficult than those beginning "what" or "who". If he's having difficulties, make things a bit easier, use simpler questions, half give the answer, and so on. Don't get upset if your child gives the "wrong" answer. Anybody who's "right" all the time won't learn anything new, after all.

General conversation Does he know the names of all the objects in the picture? Are there any he doesn't know? Can you explain them easily to him? Are you able to talk about them for long enough to hear him using them correctly again later? Encourage your child to do his fair share of talking and avoid dominating the conversation yourself. It's important to give the child time and space to express his own ideas, and you will be able to judge how fast he is learning by how long he wants the conversation to continue. Picture Points and Talking Points: Does he talk about all the points? Does he talk about anything you have done together which related to one of the picture points?

Learning Skills How many of the questions can your child manage and how long do you take to talk about each question? Which sorts of questions went well and which badly? How important is it for your child that you and he take turns being the questioner? In general, the longer he wants, the more he is learning.

Playing When your child starts playing, do you happen to hear any of the things you were talking about come out again? Could you link this into your next session with the pictures? Could you extend it with a visit to an appropriate place – castle, beach, museum, supermarket, roadworks or whatever?

Warning Perhaps the most important point is that if your child is not enjoying his sessions with you and the books he probably won't learn anything that will do him much good. The same will be true if you're not enjoying it. It is quite possible to train your child to do all sorts of things he doesn't really want to do and to force yourself through the agonies of doing so. It is very doubtful whether either of you will gain much by this.

Reading And Counting

Between the ages of three and six your child will start simple counting and is quite likely to start wanting to read. Like every other parent, you will probably be torn between wanting to teach your child more, worrying that he does not seem to be as advanced as the last child you met, and fearing that whatever you do may conflict with what the teachers will do when your child reaches school.

The Let's Learn Method

The *Let's Learn* books offer you a middle road between these various pitfalls. In the first place, they will help you to get your child ready to learn. As you share these books, your child will be learning in a thoroughly enjoyable way and will, quite automatically, want to get more involved. Secondly, you should realize that children acquire all intellectual skills very gradually and that no two children gain them in exactly the same order. These books help you to build on your child's strengths and successes and so help him to develop in an entirely natural way.

Starting to read

The best way you can help your child to begin reading is to make sure that he speaks his language fluently and understands what's said to him. He will then be far more likely to attach the appropriate meaning to the words and sentences he will find in reading books. There are other activities that are helpful before your child learns to read properly and many of these have been suggested at various places in the books. He will probably begin to recognize words that you may have pointed out to him, for example, the names of shops. Play as many word-spotting games as you like; spotting words that already mean things to him is much easier for your child than recognizing single letters, which can mean very little. If your child falls naturally into reading, then encourage him to carry on, but don't worry if he doesn't

Counting

Teaching children numbers is at least as worthwhile as helping them to start reading. A range of early number skills that you can perfectly well practise and develop have been suggested through the books. Children who have plenty of practice in the kind of skills suggested will find arithmetic and maths easier when they get to school, regardless of whether they are taught by the traditional methods or by the so-called "new maths".

Once your child has started coming to grips with the ideas in a picture, he needs to start exploring them in ways that are not just factual or intended to help him acquire solid information. He needs to play with the ideas, perhaps build fantasies round them and, whenever possible, explore them through his own activity. Some of the ideas in these pages may prove so easy for your child that they fail to interest him; others may be beyond him at present. You should be able to adapt most of them to suit your child's particular level of understanding without any difficulty.

Telling a Story

The stories are written to give you the skeleton of a story which is complete in itself, but which can easily be adapted to suit your child better. Read the story yourself very quickly first so that you can see whether it seems basically suitable or not. Try to get your child interested in the story by changing the names of the characters and locations to those of your child's and his friends, by bringing him into the story as often as you can, and by acting yourself. All children love participating in a story. Get your child to guess what might happen next, make appropriate sound effects, invent an ending for the story and so on. Go along with your child's ideas and let him produce his own version of the story. You will find that your child expects the story to make sense and you can encourage him to interrupt if it doesn't seem to do so. Don't read the stories out flatly; bring as much expression to them as you can. If the story calls for a sneeze, your child deserves the biggest, most exaggerated sneeze you have ever made followed by the chance to make one himself. Add gestures, grimaces, face pullings and so on wherever they seem appropriate. You may feel that all this drama is simply foolish, but your audience will not. He will just be thinking what a wonderful storyteller you are and how much fun he is having, listening and joining in.

Play and Learn

The games and projects are all easy to organize quickly and don't involve you in an enormous amount of preparation. This is not only to save you time, but also because young children want to do things now, not when you have spent two hours getting them ready. The suggestions can readily be adapted and made harder or easier to suit your child's interests and abilities. The games very often give you the chance to check what your child has learned about any subject by listening to what he talks about while he plays and the instructions he gives you when you join in.

STORIES GAMES AND STUDY BOXES

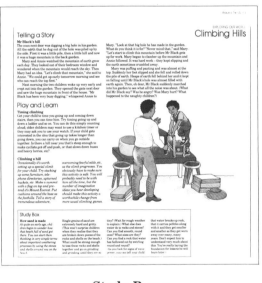

Study Boxes

These have been included for those children who want more information or who seem ready to move towards the more formal exercises that they will meet in school. Do not attempt them unless your child has enjoyed all the other activities on the subject, because you will run the risk of forcing him into something he is not ready to do. Nothing is more likely to put him off doing it for ever. Although some of the exercises we have suggested look quite formal, they can easily be made enjoyable. Very many children find that learning is fun and a great deal of evidence suggests that they learn well and quickly while they enjoy it.

Drawing, modelling and writing

It's very easy to make mistakes about children's drawing and modelling. From the start, your child will want to make things, but he will not necessarily set out to produce a realistic picture or model. You should not expect him to do so. He will tell you what he is doing and the first stage in early drawing might well be called "Naming the scribble." "Here's our house," he says and you see a mess. Then you see a darker mess inside the first mess. "That's me coming out to see you," he says. If you say, "Well, it doesn't look much like a house to me", you are on the way to depriving the world of another budding artist! Let him tell you what he is drawing, encourage him, and give him new materials to try out. Finally, let him draw and model in a place where you won't spoil everything by being annoyed when you find that he has made a mess.

As your your child gets older he will want to draw you, or the cat, or an elephant. Again, he is neither skilled enough to do it realistically nor will that be what he is attempting. He will be trying to draw an elephant in the way that is right for him now. He will draw the bit which interests him biggest and he may almost forget about the rest of the picture. Don't correct this; after all, it took most of the world's artists years of study before they could realistically draw all the things that your child wants to draw right now.

Your child's approach to model-making will be very similar. At this stage, it is much more important to let him try making models in as many different materials as you can provide than to worry about whether the results realistically represent the objects he says he is modelling.

The beginnings of writing are much the same as the beginning of drawing. Scribbling leads to making more definite strokes and then to early letters, some capitals, some small, which are all sorts of sizes and shapes. Some may even be back to front or upside down. Don't worry too much about this; give him a model letter so that he gets an idea of what he is aiming for, even though his first approximations may be wide of the mark.

Praise

Finally, in all these activities don't be halfhearted about praising your child. Make sure you give him plenty of chances to succeed. When he does, or when you know that he has tried hard, give him your generous and warm praise. He will gain confidence and try to win more praise.

CHILDREN'S PLAY

In The Sandpit

Telling a Story

Mandy's sandcastle

Today was the day when the sand was just right for castle building. Dad helped Mandy build up a big mound and then she began to smooth it down. She made a square castle with turrets, and she decorated it with shells and seaweed . . . Mandy made the finest castle on the beach.

Jim came back from a rock pool dragging his net behind him.

"Watch out!" yelled Mandy. "You nearly knocked my castle down!"

Then a dog came rushing up. "Shoo!" shouted Mandy.

Nearby some big boys were playing ball and their ball came straight by. The boys ran after it.

"Oh, no!" screamed Mandy. But at the last minute they saw the castle and jumped right over it.

"I don't know why you're working so hard," said Jim, who hadn't caught anything at all at the pool. "There's something coming that's going to knock your castle flat, and there's nothing you can do about it." Jim pointed behind her at the sea, creeping closer and closer.

"Never mind, Mandy," said Dad. He picked her up and put her right on top of the castle. She glared at the sea.

"Go away!" shouted Mandy. "Go away! I'm Queen of the Castle, and I'm ordering you to go away!" But did it go? No! It just kept creeping closer and closer. And Mandy soon had to jump back off the castle before it was too late.

Next day they all went back to the same spot and what do you think they found? Just a beach, with lots and lots of flat, golden sand.

Play and Learn

Egg-timers

Children love watching egg-timers, and all kinds of work can be done with them. Even if children cannot tell the time they can see how long the sand takes to run out by counting the minute marks on the clock face. Is the egg done exactly how your child likes it after that much time? What else can he do for that amount of time? Can he judge how long he has to keep his eyes shut and then open them just as the sand runs out? If you haven't got an egg-timer, put some sand into an old detergent bottle and let it run through the nozzle.

Salt drawings

Salt is cheap and there's usually plenty of it, so it makes a good medium for early drawings. Put the salt in a pot with a small hole and give your child a tray, or, better still, an easily cleaned floor. Encourage him to "draw" long lines, circles, squiggles, etc, with the salt. You may feel that these suggestions will simply result in a mess, but watch your child at work. He will see the lines develop, and his hand and wrist movements will change according to the shape he is making. This is all good early writing, reading and drawing experience and most children will enjoy it.

Study Box

Grains

Children are often fascinated by tiny things, so take this opportunity to capitalize on that interest. There are some ideas here for working with different substances which all consist of grains of some kind but which differ in other basic properties.

Grains What else apart from sand is made up of tiny grains? (Rice, sugar, salt are all possibilities.) Are the grains all the same size? (Try sieving rice and sugar, etc.) Can you seen any differences if you look at the grains through a magnifying glass? (You may need quite a strong lens.)

Size Just how small is a grain? Can you chop a single grain in half? Can you grind it down? Which is easier to grind, sugar or sand? Take the smallest pinch of salt, sand, sugar, rice, you can. How many grains in each pinch?

Wetness What happens if you put salt, sand or sugar into cups of warm water and stir? Which dissolve? Which don't? Can you build with damp salt or sugar? What happens if you pour a little water on to a pile of salt? (Don't expect your child to know why it happens.)

Telling a Story

Marnie's ramp

Marnie and Nicky were playing with their toy cars. Nicky built a bridge by piling up some blocks and putting a plank across the gap.

"That's silly," said Marnie. "There isn't anywhere for the bridge to go to."

"Yes, there is," said Nicky, as he put some toy cows on top of his bridge. "This is one of those bridges for animals to cross big roads. They're going to new fields with all the traffic running under them." And he pushed his biggest lorry under the bridge. "Brrmm, brmm . . ."

Marnie always liked to do things bigger and better. She was building a huge ramp for her cars.

"They'll go miles when I let them go," she said.

"I bet they won't," said Nicky. "The ramp's crooked.

They'll fall off before they get to the bottom."

"You always think you know best," said Marnie, "but I bet they go round the curve and shoot right across the floor."

She put a car right up on top and gave it a little push. It shot down the ramp, leapt over the side and hurtled across the floor.

"Look out!" yelled Nicky. But it was too late. The car shot into the bridge at top speed and knocked into a brick very hard. There was a great crash. When Marnie and Nicky opened their eyes, all they could see was a huge pile of bricks and cars and cows. Marnie looked at Nicky. Nicky looked at Marnie. Marnie giggled. Nicky giggled. And they both began to laugh.

Play and Learn

Sorting and grouping

Collect all the toy cars together for an exercise in sorting and grouping. Suggest to your child that she lines them all up with the biggest at one end, then the next biggest and so on to the smallest at the other end. Then try another line of cars with her favourite at one end and her least favourite at the other; or she might like to group them according to colour, type and so on. Even in these simple games you'll hear your child making choices and giving reasons for those choices. "I like this one better than that one because . . . that one's the slowest," etc.

Rolling games

As children begin to play rolling games with marbles, balls and other round objects, they will begin to appreciate certain ideas about movement. Try putting two books under a pair of table legs to make the table slope slightly. Don't make the slope too steep or everything will happen too quickly. Put other books or suitable objects on the table to make passages. Then give the children marbles to roll down the slope. Let them roll several at once. It's even more fun if you can arrange for the marbles to bang into something noisy, like a tin tray, at the end of their obstacle course.

Study Box

Having collisions

Set up a variety of collisions between toy cars and ask older children what they think will happen to the cars each time. It's probably too early for them to learn why it happens, but most children are bound to enjoy this early experimentation.

What will happen if . . .

One car is still	and another car runs into its front?
One car is still	and another car runs into its back?
One car is still	and another car runs into its side?
Two cars end to end and touching each other are still	and another car runs into the back of one of them?

IMAGINATIVE PLAY
Playing With Puppets

Telling a Story

Poor toys!
The toys were all in a heap in the box where Avril and Peter had thrown them at the end of the day.

"Oooh, my back," said the drum. "If that boy beats me any harder, I think he'll come right through. Couldn't you slow him up a bit, you sticks?"

"We can't really," said the sticks. "He seems to be getting better and better at it every day."

"What about me?" clattered the toy typewriter. "That girl keeps on banging all my keys down at once and getting me all stuck up. It really hurts."

"That's nothing," said the glove puppet. "Do you know what the two of them decided to play today? Crabs and lobsters! And I was meant to be the littlest crab. I thought I was going to be pinched black and blue."

"Well I think you're all lucky," whistled the mouth organ. "At least they played with you. I've been sitting in the box all day and they haven't even picked me up. And I thought they liked playing tunes on me."

"Do you call those things tunes?" grumbled the rag doll. "If you could get them to play a tune we'd be happy."

"I like the music I make," said the mouth organ. "I hope I get a turn tomorrow. At least they always blow me nice and loud."

"Yes, that's the trouble," said the glove puppet. "We want a rest tomorrow. Keep it quiet, will you?"

"Anyone would think you lot don't like being toys," said the mouth organ as they fell asleep. Would you like to be a toy?

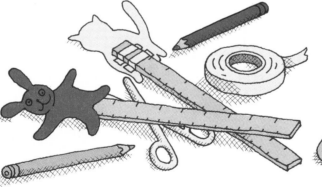

Play and Learn

Making puppets
The simplest way to make a puppet is to paint eyes and a mouth on your hand with lipstick or "face paints", using the space between your thumb and forefinger for the mouth. That's usually quite enough to get children started. You can go on to make sock or glove puppets together by fixing buttons and a few strands of wool to old socks, gloves or other discarded clothes. Simple stick puppets can be made out of any piece of wood, some material to hide the hand and act as a skirt, and an old doll's face or painted ping-pong ball for the head.

Puppet play
Fix two very rough figures on to small pieces of wood or card. They really don't need to be particularly well made at this stage. Your child will quickly give them each a name and, probably, a personality. Show her how to poke the puppets up above the back of a chair or sofa and act out a short play for you. Many children will use this kind of game to talk about worries they might not want to discuss with you directly. Don't interrupt; you may learn about unsuspected problems.

Study Box

Developing conversations
After conversations with you, playing with puppets is one of the best language development aids your child can have. It is also a useful means of working out relationships between people. The likely line of development in this type of play is:

1 Talking to favourite dolls, teddies, etc. This can be the first inventive and imaginative activity your child undertakes.
2 Making two very simple puppets talk to each other. Your child won't be interacting with another child, but she'll be exploring her imagination.

3 Learning to manipulate stick, sock and finger puppets and beginning to give them personalities. Telling complicated stories about them.
4 Using these to put on short acts with other puppets and puppeteers, which can sometimes turn into long-running serials.

Note *Obviously development through these activities can't be systematic but you should expect your child to express many emotions through puppets and soft toys. She may, for example, act you as an appalling tyrant, handing out terrible punishments for minor misdemeanours.*

Dressing Up

Telling a Story

Good guy or bad guy?
(This is a good opportunity to discuss the difference between what is real and what is simply make-believe. Children may find the distinction blurred, especially if they watch a lot of television.)

Leroy and Wayne were playing "Cowboys and Indians" in the park. They enjoyed dressing up in special clothes and tearing round the garden chasing each other. They took it in turns to be the good guy chasing the bad guy who was caught and tied up. Leroy put on a big black hat, a belt with a shiny buckle, a sheriff's badge and a black patch over his eye to make him look fierce, and he carried a piece of old rope for a lasso. Wayne liked to paint his face with bright colours and stick red and green feathers in his hair. He had an Indian costume, which he had been given for his birthday. When they were dressed up they both looked very, very fierce.

"Right," said Leroy to Wayne. "You start running and I'll catch you and tie you to that tree. Then I'll have you just where I want you."

Now Wayne was a better runner than Leroy and he was very quiet when he was hiding. He dashed off round the corner and hid behind a tree. Soon Leroy ran past yelling "Stop him! I'm going to turn him into mincemeat!"

A few minutes later Leroy ran back again, past Wayne, who was safe behind his tree. Leroy stopped. Where was Wayne? This game wasn't going to be much fun if he disappeared and refused to be tied up.

Just then Wayne's little sister Angie came up holding a ball. She wanted to play catch with her brother. She thought Leroy looked awfully frightening.

"What are you doing?" she asked.

"I'm looking for Wayne, who is a horrible Indian, and when I catch him I'm going to tie him to a tree and then go home and leave him in the park all night."

Angie turned red. She stuck out her fist and hit Leroy in the eye.

"Ow, owww!" yelled Leroy. "Why did you do that?"

"You leave my brother alone," said Angie, "or I'll do it again."

"I was only pretending," said Leroy, "and now I've got a real black eye!"

Play and Learn

Starting a costume collection
Find some things around the house and start a dressing-up box. Once you begin a collection, your child will join in and try things on. Old hats, shoes and jewellery, sunglasses, badges, etc, are a good way to start and shirts, an old curtain, headscarf, belts and safety-pins are all useful items too. You can quickly make helmets out of small cardboard boxes. Allow your child to try on as many different combinations of clothes as he likes. When your child says that he is, for example, a bus driver, co-operate by being the passenger.

Colouring dolls
Children always enjoy colouring cardboard figures. It's more exciting to colour figures they have watched you cut out specially for them. Agree who the figures are and leave your child to "dress" them by using crayons to colour clothes on. Younger children will probably just make marks, but older ones may produce recognizable divisions between trousers and jumpers and so on. Your cardboard figures do not have to be very realistic ones for this game.

Study Box

Who wears what?
Children quickly begin to learn that you can tell what people do by what they wear – especially in films. Try giving them the clues here and see if they can supply the right character. You could incorporate people from the real world: nurse, policeman, etc.

Costume	Character	Costume	Character
Cocked hat, black patch over eye, sword	Pirate	Painted face, big shoes, baggy trousers	Clown
Long leather trousers, checked shirt, lasso	Cowboy	Pointed hat, long cloak, broomstick	Witch
Big black cape, mask, pistols	Bandit/ Highwayman	Special wand, pointed hat, long cloak	Magician

Doctors And Nurses

Play and Learn

Hospital props

Your child will probably be keen to play "Doctors and Nurses" or "Hospitals" after seeing this picture. Encourage him to have a go at each of the different roles and help him prepare some simple props, eg old white jacket or coat, face mask, bandages, simple slings for toys, a plaster for a broken foot (made from a wellington boot wrapped in white paper).

Home-made bandages

Make different lengths of bandage, using cotton wool and sticky tape, and attach them to the side of a low table or chair so that your child can easily reach them as he gives his toys first-aid. The game will be even more fun if the cotton wool has red "blood" (spots of paint) added. If your child enjoys bandaging his toys he might well ask you to bandage him or decide to go out and bandage his friends. If *this is the case, use old bits of material or bandage rather than the sticky tape, which is not very pleasant against the skin.*

Telling a Story

First-aid for Teddy

Kate was very proud of her teddy bear and when Uncle Edward gave her enough money to buy him a purple and pink jacket and some bright green trousers he looked extra smart. His name was .... (let your child provide a suitable name).

One warm afternoon Kate had just put her teddy out under the apple tree for a doze while she had her lunch, when Dad arrived home early from the office. He was talking to Mum and Kate heard him say, "When I was coming up the road I saw that horrible dog from next door running down the street with something pink and purple and green in its mouth ..."

"TEDDY!" (or whatever name your child has given it) screamed Kate, jumping up and spilling her drink. "Teddy – he's gone! That was poor Teddy! He's been taken by a cruel dog."

Straight away Kate's dad got into the car and drove round looking for the dog. Sometimes he would just catch sight of it disappearing round a corner, but he could never catch up with it because the dog was so clever at jumping over walls or diving into bushes. Finally Dad did catch up with the dog as it was sitting down having a rest in .... (a place known to your child). But the naughty dog no longer had Kate's teddy! Dad drove home and told Kate the sad news. "Oh – he must have eaten him," sobbed Kate. "I wish I'd never left him under the apple tree."

At that moment, however, there was a knock on the door and a policeman came in holding a battered teddy. "I found him in the gutter and brought him straight home," he said. "I hope you didn't miss him."

"Oh thank you, thank you, thank you!!!" cried Kate. And she quickly bathed Teddy's scratches with warm water, put his hurt arm in a sling and a plaster on his bumped head. Then she took his temperature with a .... (see if your child knows the word). That's right, with a thermometer, and popped him into bed.

"It was lucky your teddy had his name and address in his jacket," said the policeman, "or I wouldn't have known where to bring him." Do you know your name and address? Let's practise saying it right now. And what about your telephone number?

Study Box

Safety

Children need to be watched carefully when they are playing "Doctors and Nurses". There are some firm rules, which you should make sure they understand and keep. If the game is supervised children can learn a good deal about first-aid.

1 Make sure any "medicine" really is something drinkable and not a poisonous mixture. Don't put the "medicine" into real medicine bottles. Children must learn never to touch medicine or pill bottles.
2 Do not allow children to poke their fingers into each other's ears or eyes.

3 Make sure they don't want to put small objects into ears or noses.
4 If children want to perform operations, let them do so on a toy and not on each other.
5 Children always enjoy comparing their cuts and grazes, etc. They like to boast about the size of the injury

and how much it hurt, and to detail the treatment they received. (That is a good opportunity to check how much proper first-aid they know.) You can lead them on to discuss whether they could have avoided getting hurt. (See ABOUT OUR BODIES, p. 42.)

Pirates

Telling a Story

Jake Carlson's treasure

Once upon a time there was a bold and fierce pirate called Jake Carlson. He roamed the seas for many years attacking and robbing ships carrying treasure from South America to Spain. On his last voyage he was shipwrecked on a small island in the Caribbean Sea and he lived there alone for three years. Luckily, Jake Carlson had been quite good at being a pirate and so it didn't take him long to make himself a hut and a fishing line and to find out which of the plants that grew on the island could be eaten. And in between whiles he dug himself a deep, deep hole. Then one day a ship stopped at the island and Jake was rescued by the sailors.

He didn't dare tell the ship's crew that he was a pirate because pirates were sent to prison or killed if they were caught. So he told them he was an ordinary sailor and indeed he worked as an ordinary sailor until he grew too old to go to sea.

When he was old and about to die he told a little girl, who lived in the same house, that he had buried some treasure on that Caribbean island in that deep, deep hole. He said he had a map that showed where the island was and he had put a cross to mark the hole where he had hidden the treasure. He told her to take the map after he died. He hoped that when she grew up she would sail the seas and find his treasure.

I don't know if the little girl did find the treasure when she grew up or not. Perhaps it is still buried in the hole on that little island waiting to be found. What do you think?

Play and Learn

Making up a game

When children start enjoying the kind of pretending play shown in this picture, the most helpful thing you can do is to make sure that they are provided with plenty of suitable props that they can sort out themselves. You can suggest that boats need sails, oars, flags, etc, and that pirates need patches, hats and swords, but leave the children to decide how they will use what. As they tackle these problems they will find that they are building a story around the props and so the preparation will become an important part of the creative process.

Drawing maps

If your child is inspired by the story, she might like to follow it up by drawing and colouring a real "treasure map", showing where Jake Carlson buried his pieces of eight. She will need to know the conventions of such maps, such as the fact that a cross usually marks the spot where treasure is buried and that different areas of a treasure island are often given colourful names: Tall Tree Hill, Fishy Bay, Coconut Cove, etc. She can be encouraged to show the sea around the island, wooded areas, a stream, etc. She could supply a list of clues and get you to guess where the treasure is.

Study Box

Villains' language
Children enjoy learning specialized phrases that are always associated with particular activities – "Stick 'em up", for example. They use them in their games and often outside them as well. Do they know these and who says them?

Saying	Characters	Saying	Characters
Shiver mi' timbers	Pirates	Stand and deliver	Highwaymen
Walk the plank	Pirates	Reach, mister	Cowboys
I'm going to change you into a . . .	Evil magicians	Hubble, bubble, toil and trouble	Witches

Party Games

Telling a Story

The new party game

"Auntie Janet, what game are we going to play?" asked Johnny on the morning of his party. He was very pleased Auntie Janet was there. She always had such good ideas.

"You'll see," smiled Auntie Janet. "First of all, can you make me a fan for each child coming to the party by folding sheets of newspaper?"

While Johnny did that, wondering furiously what the game could be, Auntie Janet made some large fish shapes out of tissue paper.

"The game's called 'Fan the Kipper'," said Auntie Janet, but Johnny couldn't think what that could be.

Well, the children all arrived, and soon it was time to play Auntie Janet's game. The children were divided into two teams and four from each side were sent to one end of the room and four were kept at the other. When Dad gave the signal, the first two children, one from each team, had to fan the tissue paper fishes across the floor, using the paper fans. Oh, it was fun! The paper kippers flipped about all over the place. The children soon discovered how careful they had to be if they wanted their kipper to go in the right direction.

When they got across the floor the next person in the team fanned the kipper back to the beginning again. The children in the team did this until everybody in the team had had a turn. Johnny was disappointed that his team did not win but Dad said they could play again after they had all had a drink of lemonade. They certainly needed it. What an exciting game!

Play and Learn

Participation games

"O'Grady says" is an excellent game that encourages everyone to take part without demanding too much from the shy ones. Choose someone to be O'Grady, who gives commands by saying "O'Grady says ... put your hands in the air." Children need to listen carefully because they're out if they don't do it. Older children can be told only to do things which O'Grady says. Anyone who obeys a command not prefixed by the phrase "O'Grady says" has been tricked into being out. The little ones will just enjoy following the commands. There is no need to be so strict with them.

Home-made games

Try inventing some very simple games and getting your children to make up the rules. Simple skittles can be played by piling up bricks, saucepan lids, etc, and rolling a ball at them. You may need rules about how far away you can throw from, how many turns you can have, etc. The only prize you need is the immensely satisfying noise of a direct hit! Ping-pong football involves two children blowing a ping-pong ball into each other's goals (upturned cups). Don't intervene too quickly when you hear a cry of "that's not fair". It's best if they can sort things out themselves.

Study Box

Getting ready

These are some favourite party games, but your children may know some others. Let them suggest a few and then work out all the things you would need before you start. Let them help you prepare the games for a party at home.

Game	What you need
Blind Man's Buff	Blindfold
Musical chairs	Several chairs, music source
Pass-the-parcel	Present, lots of paper, music source
Pin-the-tail-on-the-donkey	Reasonably well-drawn donkey, tail, backing that's easy to push pin into

Hide And Seek

Telling a Story

Mr Hide and Miss Seek

Mr Hide was a very funny man. He pulled faces like this (pull some funny faces) at people. Every day he went out to pull funny faces at people in the street. Sometimes they thought he was funny and sometimes they didn't.

Miss Seek was a very funny woman. She pulled faces like this (pull a different funny face) at people.

One warm summer's day Mr Hide thought to himself: "As it's such a nice day, I think I shall go out to the other side of the town and meet some new people to pull faces at." And on the very same day Miss Seek thought happily to herself:

"As it's such a sunny day I think I shall go out and do some funny face-pulling." She met lots of people to pull funny faces at: the butcher, the baker (mention some people your child knows), and soon got right to the middle of the town. Miss Seek was never happier than when she was pulling plenty of funny faces.

All of a sudden Miss Seek saw a man she had never seen before. Who do you think it was?

"Ah ha!" she thought. "There's someone new to surprise with a funny face." So she drew in her cheeks and curled up her nose and puffed out her lips and pulled the funniest face she'd ever made. (Can your child imagine how it must have looked?) It was such an effort that Miss Seek was quite out of breath.

And you know who it was she was making her funny face at, don't you? Yes, it was Mr Hide. And when Mr Hide saw her he squashed up his nose and sucked in his lips and closed his eyes, wriggled his ears and pulled the funniest face in the whole world.

Miss Seek was so surprised that her mouth dropped open and she dropped her shopping. And then she started laughing and so did Mr Hide, so much that he dropped his shopping too. Well, they became firm friends and very soon they decided they would get married and live together and teach each other all their funny faces.

They had a wonderful wedding party where all their friends danced and sang and ate. And they both invented a brand new hiding game to play with their friends. No one had ever played it before but lots of people have played it since. Can you guess what it was called?

Play and Learn

Hide and seek variations

If you can't face a full-scale, human hide and seek game in the house, try a scaled-down version using dolls, teddies or other favourite toys, taking it in turns with your child to be hider and seeker. Start with easy places, or you may find she gets discouraged, but you can soon go on to more imaginative places as she gets the idea. This is a useful thinking exercise as well as fun.

"Find-the-mice"

This is a hiding game that can be played quietly. It's called "Find-the-mice". Take an old, well-illustrated magazine and draw a number of small mice in the margins, in the middle of adverts or hidden somewhere in other illustrations. Give your child coloured pencils and ask her to find the mice and ring them. Some children will need to find the mice easily, but you can make this a difficult game if your child enjoys it. Let her hide some mice for you to find so that she can think about how best to conceal them.

Study Box

Name the rules

Ask your child if she knows the rules of these and other games. Can she explain exactly how to play? Ask questions by pretending you want to play but don't know how to. Ask older children about more complicated games.

Indoor games		Outdoor games	
Pass-the-parcel	Hunt-the-thimble	Pig-in-the-middle	Hopscotch
Musical chairs	Snakes and Ladders	French cricket	Tennis
Blind Man's Buff	Tiddlywinks	Rounders	Football
Snap	Beg-o-my-neighbour	Any skipping game	Any running game

KEEPING RULES

Indoor Games Play and Learn

I spy

Play a game of "I spy" using this picture as a starting point and different games as the objects you are spying. For example, "I spy a game that needs two people, a black and white checked board and black and white counters. What is it?" Give similar clues for Snakes and Ladders, Dominoes and Patience. When the alternatives in the picture have been exhausted, make the game harder by turning it into an "I'm thinking of . . ." activity, where the visual clues are missing. Describe games you have at home or that your child knows, and let him guess what they are.

Card houses

Follow up the Learning Skills (p. 23). Work on shapes by getting out sets of dominoes, cards, chessmen, etc, and encouraging your child to build with them. Younger children will need to use the firmer pieces, but older children can work *quite carefully to see if they can combine cards and dominoes, put chess pieces on top of a card house, etc. Children always enjoy this kind of activity and it's one that encourages them to practise being careful with their hands.*

Telling a Story

Unlucky black

One wet, dark afternoon Michael and Dad sat down to play a game of Draughts together. Michael had only just learned how to play and he liked playing whenever there was a spare minute.

Michael chose to play with the black pieces because black was his lucky colour and anyway, white always starts and Michael preferred to have second go. It gave him more time to think.

Soon the game was going well for Michael. Although Dad had won a few black pieces, Michael had won a lot more white ones.

Then Dad moved a piece to the right, and Michael saw his chance.

"If I go there this turn," thought Michael, "I'll be able to go there next turn and take that one and that one and that one."

He felt very excited as he pushed his piece forwards. He could hardly wait for Dad to move again so that he could take all Dad's pieces.

But to his surprise, Dad started chortling in a very smug way. He even waved his arms in the air and said "Ah ha! I've trapped you." And he picked up a white piece that Michael had hardly noticed and jumped over Michael's black piece and then over another and another. Three pieces gone!

Now Dad had won more pieces than Michael and there were more white pieces than black pieces left on the board. Soon Dad had won the game.

Michael felt upset because he had been so sure he was going to win. He didn't want to be a bad sport but he had a funny feeling inside which made it very difficult for him to smile. He did smile though.

"I never saw that piece," he said. "Black certainly wasn't my lucky colour today."

"You didn't look hard enough to see what moves I might make because you were thinking too much about your own," said Dad. "And it's not really luck, is it?"

Michael soon cheered up and started laying out all the pieces again, ready for another game.

"Right, come on. Let's see if I can trap you this time. You'd better watch out," he said to his dad.

Study Box

Board games	Rules	Cheating	
Snakes and Ladders	Simple	Possible by moving counter too far	*Ask your child to list the important points about any board games he knows. Can he add to the lists here and then think about other games as well? An intelligent game of chess may be beyond him, but most children enjoy learning how the different pieces move.*
Draughts	Quite hard	Possible if opponent isn't looking	
Chess	Complicated	Impossible. Opponent knows your moves	

Outdoor Games

Telling a Story

Jane's new team-mates

Every Tuesday Jane went to the playground to play football with her friends. They always met each other at the place where there was a goal painted on the wall and they took it in turns to be goalkeeper while the others kicked the ball. Jane could kick as hard as the biggest boys and girls but she didn't like being goalkeeper because the ball always seemed to go between her legs.

One Tuesday two boys were there who Jane had never seen before. They had red shirts and white shorts and proper football boots too.

"Look at them," said Billy. "I bet they're good!"

"Well I'm not playing with them," said Jane, who was wearing her usual jeans and sneakers. "They're strangers, and anyway, they're much too clean."

"Cleany, cleany," she called out at the boys. And soon all the other children were calling out at them too. In the end, the boys just went away. "Good," said Jane. "Now we can all get on with our game."

The very next day, Jane was walking through the park when she saw a game of football starting. She went up to the players and asked, "Can I play?" One of them turned round and Jane gasped. It was one of the "cleanies", and he was captain of his side.

"Well, we do want some more players," said the boy, "but you don't like playing with us, do you?"

Jane went red. She felt awful. When it was half-time she went up to the captain and said she was sorry. Then she started to walk home very sadly. Suddenly she heard steps behind her, and a voice said:

"Come on then, we'd like you to play after all." How do you think Jane felt then?

Play and Learn

Poker face

This is an easy game, requiring no props, only a large degree of self-control and concentration. Each child takes it in turn to sit absolutely still and not laugh or smile. She must keep her eyes open, but she can look wherever she likes. The other players try to make her laugh. They can do anything except touch the poor victim. The trick is not to think about what is going on in the room.

Follow-the-leader

This is a very simple game which very young children can join in too. Select one person to be the leader (it may have to be you to begin with). Everyone else must copy what the leader does. The leader should change actions fairly often so that the followers have to keep on the alert. Very young children may have difficulty mimicking the actions of someone older, but this kind of game will help their co-ordination. The older the children, the more difficult the game can be.

Study Box

About rules

Even if you feel your children are too young to be expected to understand the rules of complicated games, you will find that they will easily absorb a number of general ideas about playing with others by being included by older brothers and sisters.

Rule	Game (example)	Rule	Game (example)
You can't change the rules once you've started playing	All games	The person who finishes with the highest score wins	Marbles
Some people are on your side, and some are on the other	Team games, eg football	You have to take turns at doing the most exciting part	Skipping

KEEPING RULES
Football

Play and Learn

Rules

It's obviously important for children to understand why rules exist for games as soon as possible, because it will help them to join in all kinds of games successfully and will further their ability to get on with other children. It is often more productive, however, to approach the subject in a positive way rather than to list the "don'ts" that apply to any particular game. Let your child choose a favourite game and ask her to talk through how it is played: what the object of the game is; how many people play; what is allowed and what is not allowed, etc.

Kick and aim

Long before they can understand the rules of football and the intricacies of the game, children will enjoy just kicking a ball around. To help them realize some of the skills involved in the game, get them to try and manoeuvre a large ball to a specific spot, without using their hands. They'll soon learn that it's not just a matter of swiping at it.

Telling a Story

Tim's first game

Tim was five and he had a big brother called John who was eight. Tim and John thought that football was the best game in the world. But while John played in a boys' football team with his friends, Tim was only allowed to watch from the edge of the pitch.

"You're too young, Tim," they told him when he begged to be allowed to join in. "You can't play football when you are only five – that's still a baby."

Poor Tim, he watched every game that John played. He cheered John when he played well and ran to fetch the ball when it was kicked off the pitch. But watching wasn't the same as playing, was it? Tim just couldn't wait three years until he was eight. He wanted to play so much.

After watching lots of football matches Tim got to know what each player was doing – he watched their moves carefully and then practised for himself in the back garden. He learned how to trap the ball, and dribble, and pass it to another player. Sometimes when Dad wasn't busy he would play with Tim. Dad thought Tim played well. "You will be a good footballer when you are eight, Tim," he said, patting him on the head.

One Saturday morning there was an important match. John's team was playing the football team from another village. The game started well and the other team had scored one goal when one of the boys who played striker for John's team fell and hurt his leg. It was no good, he couldn't play any more and he limped off the pitch. What could they do? Suddenly the referee turned to Tim and asked him to play instead. He had to borrow some football boots, but his T-shirt was nearly the right colour for the team. Tim ran happily on to the football pitch and everyone cheered and clapped.

The players were much bigger and kicked harder than Tim did, but he ran and ran and tried as hard as he could. Near the end he was so tired that he could hardly run any more. Just then somebody kicked the ball really hard. It was shooting past the goal but Tim was in the way. It thudded against his feet, twisted past the goalkeeper and shot in between the posts. "GOAL!" everybody shouted. "Tim's saved the game!"

Tim never forgot his first game.

Study Box

Ball games: equipment

Children who are interested in games can help you to draw up an illustrated chart about them. Here are a few suggestions. It should not be difficult to find pictures to cut out. Finish it off by adding favourite players.

Sport	Equipment	Protection	Judge
Football	Boots, goals	Shin pad	Referee, linesmen
Cricket	Bat, stumps	Gloves, pads	Umpires
Baseball	Bat	Glove, helmet	Umpire
Hockey	Stick	Shin pads	Umpire
Rounders	Bat	None	Referee
Tennis	Racket, net	None	Umpire, line judges

Making Music

Telling a Story

Josephine and the xylophone

Josephine was a little girl who always enjoyed music. But she had no musical instruments at home to play. She used to watch all the music programmes on TV and pretend to join in with the musicians. Most of all, she wanted a chance to play on a real instrument.

Mr Brown, Josephine's teacher, liked music as well and every day in school the children would sing songs and learn to clap rhythm together. Mr Brown would say "You must try to keep in time with each other." Josephine was very good at that. They used to tap out the sounds of the children's names. (Say "You try it: Jo-se-phine, Jo-se-phine. Try your name.") She always looked forward to these times and used to practise tapping out rhythms at home. But secretly, she wanted to play the big xylophone that was kept in the school hall.

One morning, when the singing time was finished, Mr Brown went to the music cupboard. Josephine was very excited. Mr Brown said that since everyone was so good at clapping rhythms, the time had come to try playing with some instruments. First he gave out six triangles, but he didn't give one to Josephine. Then he gave out two drums, but he didn't give one to Josephine. (Continue this pattern with none for Josephine each time.) Josephine was very sad. All the others had an instrument, but the cupboard was empty and she still had nothing to play.

Do you think Mr Brown had forgotten Josephine? No, he hadn't. He had a surprise for her. He reached up to the top of the cupboard and brought down a large box.

"Come and help me open this," he said to Josephine. When Josephine took off the lid her eyes lit up.

"Let's see what you can do with this xylophone."

Play and Learn

Music games

Before they start learning an instrument, children will enjoy beating out the rhythm of nursery rhymes or other children's songs which they know well and which you may have on record. They can also blow the rhythm on a whistle or recorder even if they don't know any notes. You can teach children more about music by making a scrap-book, using pictures of instruments and musicians.

Make simple instruments
Shakers are easy to make by putting buttons, dried peas or pins into small screw-top containers and taping them up. Pitched notes can be produced by filling some bottles with different levels of water and then tapping them with a pencil. Try stretching elastic bands across a box and plucking them. All sorts of banging instruments can be devised. Try tapping various things about the house and notice the different sounds they produce. Metallic objects are good and noisy!

Study Box

Instruments
Instruments can be arranged in groups according to the way they are played. Ask children if they can name at least two instruments under each heading, and then work backwards by naming the instruments and asking how they are played.

Blowing	Hitting	Plucking	Shaking
Recorder	Drum	Guitar	Bells
Trumpet	Triangle	Violin	Tambourine
Whistle	Xylophone	Harp	Rattles
Saxophone	Cymbal	Banjo	Maracas

MUSIC AND DANCE
The Band

Telling a Story

The new band

It was a rainy day and David, Ann and Sean were bored.

"What can we do, Mum?" they asked.

"Why don't you play some records?" said Mum. So the three children got out the record player and looked for their favourite tunes to play. The picture on the front of one record was of a large band playing.

"Let's play that music," said Sean.

The music was marching tunes played by the band. The children started to tap their feet in time to the music. Then David got up and started to march around the room waving his arms up and down. The other two followed, marching smartly like soldiers.

"That was good," Mum said when the music had finished. "Look, I've brought you some instruments. Why don't you play like the band in the picture?" She showed the children the instruments. There were two saucepan lids, one comb covered with a piece of tissue paper, and a large tin filled with buttons.

"But these aren't real instruments," said Ann.

"You can play them just the same," said Mum. "Look."

First she crashed the saucepan lids (crash, crash). Then she blew through the comb and paper (brrr, brrr). Then she shook the tin of buttons (rattle, rattle). The children took the instruments. Mum switched on the marching music and with a stick she waved, she counted one, two, one, two.

The children marched and played in time to the music. They had made their very own band.

Play and Learn

Sounds and rhythm

It is not necessary to have a house full of instruments to make sounds or to play in time. You could get your children to use their hands and feet as instruments by clapping the sounds of their names (Ma-ry, Chris-to-pher) or stamping their feet to the names of various familiar objects (mo-tor-bike, ice-cream, tri-cy-cle). Let them suggest some further words to clap and stamp to; then let them try to stamp and clap at the same time. Other sounds can be made using other parts of the body: whistling, humming, snapping fingers, and so on.

Marching

Marching tunes are some of the easiest for children to keep time to, but that doesn't mean they'll be able to do it straight away. They need to practise marching, getting the correct foot and arm going forward and back together. Do this while you are out shopping, when you don't have to worry about the music as well as the rhythm. (It is a useful way of learning left from right. Get them to say "left, right" as they march along.) As they get older and more confident, children will be able to march to band music and play simple instruments (drums, cymbals, triangles) at the same time.

Study Box

Brass instruments
Once children understand that instruments fall into different categories, you can begin to explore one group to show that smaller instruments tend to make higher notes and larger instruments lower ones. Demonstrate by using an assortment of jars.

Description	Instrument	Description	Instrument
Short, three valves, high sounds	Cornet	Very long, slides in and out, middle sounds	Trombone
Medium length, three valves, middle sounds	Trumpet	U-shaped, quite big, lower sounds	Euphonium
Circular, several rings, four valves, middle sounds	French horn	U-shaped, very big, very deep sounds	Tuba

Disco Dancing

Telling a Story

The twins' party

A lot of things aren't fair when you're six; especially if you've got an older brother and sister like the twins. I don't know if Sam and Kate are twelve or thirteen but they're heaps older than me and they're always telling me I can't do things till I grow up.

"We're having a party tomorrow," Sam said to me one day, "but of course you'll be fast asleep in bed."

"I just don't know which of my tapes to play," said Kate. "What a pity you won't be awake to hear them and see the dancing."

Even when Mum takes my side, it doesn't help much. But tonight I've made a plan. They've already put me to bed, but I've got up again and put on my party dress. And when I hear the music, I'm going to go right down there

and make a terrible scene if they don't let me stay.

The only thing is, I feel a bit tired just now. I think I'll lie down on the bed for a little while . . .

And so, of course, they found me in the morning lying on the bed in my crumpled party dress. You can guess what they said.

It wasn't till tea-time that Sam said, "Here's something for you." And he pulled back the cloth and there was a whole plateful of party food they'd kept specially for me.

And after that, Kate played her favourite tape and we danced together.

I felt quite good when I went to bed. They're not all bad, those twins of mine.

Play and Learn

Dancing to the beat

Mastering rhythm is an extremely important skill. If your child is going to learn to play an instrument, to sing, or to do ballet or gymnastics, he will need a good sense of timing. Listen to the rhythm of different pop songs and hum or clap to mark the beat. Then make up some steps with your child which keep in time with the music and do them together. When your child has mastered the steps, get him to mark the rhythm himself. After a while, he won't need to do it out loud and will be able to dance to all kinds of music. Let him have as wide a variety of music as you can.

Disco dancer

Once your child can move rhythmically to some extent, and if he enjoys dancing, encourage him to make up a dance routine with his friends. Choose a tune with a simple beat to start with and help them work out the routine. It doesn't matter if dancing has never been your strong point: all you

need do is suggest they work in some claps, kicks, steps to the left and right, dips and bends and a few simple arm movements. It may help them to perform in front of a mirror so they can see how each move looks. They might even like to put on a disco show for you once they've mastered their routine.

Study Box

Different dances
Children will be able to tell one sort of music from another at quite an early age. Borrow records or tapes from the library to extend your own collection if necessary and play short extracts to your child to see which go down well.

Kind of music	Instruments you hear	Dance you could do
Nursery rhyme	Piano, voice	Mime the actions
Pop and Rock	Guitar, drum, electric guitar	Rock 'n' Roll, disco
Classical	Orchestral instruments	Ballet type
Folk	Guitar, recorder, flute	Jigs, reels
Jazz	Trumpet, saxophone, clarinet, etc	Jive

PHYSICAL SKILLS
Swimming

Play and Learn

Swimming animals

What animals other than fish has your child seen swimming? Dogs? Ducks? If he has been to an aquarium or the zoo, he can probably add dolphins, penguins, sea lions, even hippos to that list. Some animals have to swim in order to catch food; some, like dogs, swim because they enjoy it. Other animals hardly ever swim. Has he ever seen a rabbit swimming, for example? Ask him to note which animals seem to swim better than people and which seem to find it hard work. Which animals have streamlined bodies? Do any swim with strokes like ours?

In the swimming pool

Before you first take your child to the pool, make sure that he is quite confident in the bath and that he doesn't mind having his face splashed or going under the shower. Spend the first few visits at the pool giving him the confidence to feel quite

safe by supporting him firmly and letting him see how well his floats work. Show him that he can always put his feet on the bottom or hang on to the side of the pool if he feels nervous or tired. Never force him into the water.

Telling a Story

Jim gets in

When Jim first went to the swimming pool he felt very, very frightened because it was so noisy! Everyone seemed to be shouting or yelling or screaming – and some big children were splashing and doing great high jumps off the diving board.

Jim blew up his arm bands, fixed them on carefully and stood at the side of the pool. "I'll count up to five and when I get to five, I'll jump in," he said. (Get children to count . . .) 1-2-3-4-5 – but he didn't jump, because the water looked too cold.

"I know," he thought, "I'll count up to ten – that will be easier. 1-2-3-4-5-6-7-8-9-TEN," he said, but still he didn't jump because the water looked so cold and splashy.

"I know," he said, "I'll count up to twenty." (Same result, etc.)

Then Jim had a good idea. "I know," he decided, "instead of jumping in, I'll slither in." So he got down on his tummy and began to slither like a snake. But the side of the pool was cold and wet and slippery . . . and when his face got near the water he thought he could see wriggly things in it. So do you know what he did?

That's right, he got up and stood there looking at the pool again. What on earth was he going to do?

At last, he decided: "I know how to get in . . . I'll shut my eyes and walk along the side until I tumble in because I won't be able to see where I'm going."

So Jim shut his eyes and began to walk. He seemed to be walking for rather a long time, and he still hadn't fallen in the water. It suddenly felt rather cold. He stopped and frowned, then opened his eyes. Do you know where he was? He had walked right out of the swimming pool area and was in the street! There he was, in his swimming trunks and arm bands and bare feet, and everyone was looking at him.

Jim felt very silly indeed. He turned and ran back towards the swimming pool and he was running so fast that he tripped up and . . . SPLASH! He fell straight into the pool! The nice warm water closed over his head. As he came up again he heard the other children shouting.

"Hurray, Hurray!" they were all shouting together. "At last! Jim's IN!"

Study Box

Special names
All sports have particular skills or movements that have special names which children like to use as they become more expert. How many of these do your children know? Can they describe them?

Word	Sport
Breaststroke, crawl, backstroke, butterfly, belly-flop, duck dive	Swimming and diving
Trot, canter, gallop	Horse riding
Serve, smash, volley, lob	Tennis/Squash
Bat, bowl, field, keep the score	Cricket
Tackle, dribble, pass, shoot	Football/Hockey
Drive, swing, chip, putt	Golf

Ice Skating

Telling a Story

Snowed up

One winter Lempi and Aarne went on holiday to the small cabin beside a lake that they usually only used in summer. Everyone was enjoying it except their dog, Pasha, because there was so much snow that he couldn't run around. But even Pasha had something to do when he found the mice in the woodshed.

Most of all Lempi and Aarne enjoyed trying out their new skates. At first, there were falls and tumbles, but one morning Lempi put on her skates, stood up and zoomed on to the ice. Soon Aarne was just as good.

One day, a cold wind blew, and the sky became very dark. It started to snow so hard they couldn't go out that day. The next day they woke up to find that the snow had stopped falling, but they would be snowed up inside their cabin until the snow plough came through. They'd have to start digging a path from the cabin to the road themselves.

What fun they had! They worked so hard that they didn't get cold and, whenever they had some breath left, they sang country songs to help speed the digging along. When they went back to the cottage for their midday meal they called for Pasha, but he did not come. Where could he be? They called and called and Dad went as far as he could into the deep snow. "Listen!" he said. They heard barking and it was coming from the woodshed. Poor Pasha! His front paw had been caught under a heavy log which must have rolled from the huge pile stored there. "Well," said Dad, "we must get help for him. His paw is hurt." Pasha lay on the floor licking his injured paw while everyone tried to decide what to do.

"How are we to do that? We are really snowed up! We'll never get round the road to the village."

"There is nothing else for it but to skate over to the village to see if there is anyone who can help." Dad set off across the ice with Pasha, carefully wrapped in a warm blanket, in the rucksack on his back.

They waited for what seemed like ages and began to get a little worried. But then they heard a shout. It was Dad. Pasha was going to be all right but he had to stay with the vet. Tomorrow the snow plough would get through to the cabin and they would all be able to go and see their pet.

Play and Learn

Investigating ice

When it is very cold outside, put a bowl of water out on the windowsill and leave it there for different lengths of time. You will probably be able to show that the ice gets thicker after longer periods in freezing conditions. Overnight in freezing temperatures will produce the thickest ice. (You could use the freezer compartment of a refrigerator or the freezer if you prefer.) Use toys or various kitchen weights to show that ice has to be really thick before it will support much weight. This is a useful way of teaching children the danger of treading on thin ice.

Sliding ice

Take a small container such as an old jam jar lid and fill it with water. Find a favourite small plastic toy and stand it in the water-filled container. Then freeze it. When the ice is solid, melt off the lid with a little warm water and let your child skim the toy across the floor or a table top. You could, of course, simply use an ice cube if you are in a hurry. Listen to what your child says as she begins to discover that ice slides in the most satisfactory way, but soon begins to melt.

Study Box

Movement words	On ice	On firm ground	On mud
Practice using those words which are particularly appropriate for describing how we move on ice. Can your child make some suggestions herself? Are the words she uses about ice appropriate to describe movement on other surfaces?	Sliding	Running	Wading
	Skating	Jumping	Wallowing
	Falling head over heels	Walking	Splashing
	Gliding	Hopping	Squelching
	Curving	Rolling	Sloshing

PHYSICAL SKILLS
Fishing

Telling a Story

Skilful Sarah

Sarah was going fishing. What's more she was going all by herself. She got up very early in the morning and got her rod out of the cupboard. She got her line ready and she carefully chose all the weights and tackle she would need. Then she went out in the garden and got the tin of bait that Dad wouldn't let her keep in the house.

Sarah said goodbye to Dad and ran down to the harbour. She was the first there and she knew the best place to go. She hurried to get there before any other anglers arrived. Then she fixed her bait on the hook and let it down into the water in her own special secret way.

She fished for quite some time and slowly other anglers began to arrive.

"That girl's been here ages," she heard them say, "and she hasn't caught anything. I bet she doesn't really know how to catch fish."

But then there was a tug on the line and Sarah jerked up the rod and started to reel in. Slowly, slowly her catch came in with the rod bending all the time. It was a big one. Sarah landed it carefully and carried it proudly home.

"You were lucky, Sarah," said her father, as he helped her prepare the fish for cooking.

"Lucky?" said Sarah. "I wasn't lucky. I spent ages getting ready and I knew just where to go and I let my line down in my own special way. That's not luck, you know, Dad, that's skill."

"Yes dear," said her father smiling. But I don't think he really believed Sarah. Would you?

Play and Learn

Fish watching

If you keep fish as pets, your children will probably enjoy observing them. Otherwise, schools, museums, some restaurants and pet shops are all places where you might find an aquarium, and it's worth spending five minutes studying the fish in detail. How do they swim? What do they do with their tails and with their other fins? Can your child see the fish breathing? (Yes, but she may not realize what it is doing.) Do they ever stop swimming? Do fish ever shut their eyes and go to sleep? (They do go to sleep but they cannot shut their eyes.)

Fishing games

First make your fish. Stuff the legs of old pairs of tights (different colours if possible) with newspaper and add rudimentary features. Perhaps a button would do for an eye. Attach a large loop to each fish and give your child a rod and line with the hook from a wire coat hanger. Younger children may want a fish permanently attached to their line so they don't get too frustrated. Older children can start up a fishing game. Use a chair or sofa as the pier. You could give the fish different numbers and see who can catch the highest score – or the most fish – in a certain time.

Study Box

Angling

Children need a fair amount of information before they can go fishing successfully. Try to get them to think out why anglers have the tackle they do, but make sure they know what they're up to before they set out on their own.

The hook is specially shaped to hold the bait and catch in the fish's mouth. It has a little flange to help it hold the fish firmly.

The weights are necessary to make sure the line sinks. Although a few fish can be caught near the surface, most are found in deeper water.

The line is tied to a small swivel, which is attached to a transparent trace that the fish can't see.

The trace is knotted (firmly) to the hook.

Bait for sea fishing can be lugworms, ragworms, or shellfish, which can all be found on the beach. Some fish will try to eat feathers and other shiny objects.

Safety is, as usual, very important. Excited anglers can forget all about deep water and slippery rocks. They should always fish with friends or where there are other anglers nearby.

A Ballet

Telling a Story

Emma the arm dancer

It was dancing lesson at school. The teacher had put on the music for the ballet "Swan Lake" and all the children except one were gliding about pretending to be swans. Emma wasn't. She sat in her wheelchair wishing and wishing that she could dance too. But her legs wouldn't work. She couldn't even stand on them – let alone dance!

The music made Emma think of what swans looked like and how they moved. She began to move her hands and arms. First she pretended one arm was a swan's long neck (all do these actions as you tell the story) – lifting its head, diving down into the water for a tasty snack, preening its feathers. She used both arms to be a swan flying. She tucked one hand under the other arm to be a swan sleeping. Then as the music became sadder she used

both hands again to show a swan getting weaker and weaker. Emma's swan sank slowly down and, when the music stopped, it died.

Then the clapping began. Emma looked up to see that some of the children had stopped dancing and had been watching her. "I didn't know you could dance with just your hands," one of them said. "Well, now you do know," said the teacher. "That was very good, Emma!"

After that, Emma always joined in the dancing lesson. She still wished she could dance with her whole body like the other children but she enjoyed her hand-dancing. Sometimes the teacher asked her to show the other children how to do it and then they all joined in and did hand-dancing together.

Play and Learn

Feet and arms

Ask young children if they can move like ballet dancers. Can they stand on one leg with their arms stretched out? Can they stand on one leg and move their arms or the other leg without falling over, or stand with heels touching and toes pointing in opposite directions? Can they stand like this and then raise their arms in a graceful arch over their heads? Don't encourage young children to stand on their "points". Their feet aren't strong enough and even ballet dancers need special shoes (see border) and lots of training before they can do it properly.

Making a ballet

As young children become more confident about moving to music, you can suggest they try to be swans and other creatures. It is not necessary for you to have the real "Swan Lake" music. "Swan Lake" is a famous ballet but how would your children move to tell the story of the less well-known

"Frog Lake" or, even, the terrifying "Snake Lake"? What kind of music would they have? You may need to give some help. Children are not professional dancers and they will need encouragement. Make sure you recognize which of their actions represents a frog, etc, and praise them for it.

Study Box

Swan Lake

Although it's not particularly important for children to know the story of "Swan Lake" before working on the picture, older children are bound to ask you about it, and it contains all the elements of a classic fairy story so they should enjoy it.

At a celebration on Prince Siegfried's twenty-first birthday, his mother tells him that he must soon marry. Siegfried's friends ask him to go hunting swans, but they are so beautiful that he watches them instead. One of the swans changes into a beautiful woman. She tells Siegfried

that she is Odette, a princess who has been bewitched by the evil magician and turned into the Queen of the Swans. She can only turn back if a prince vows to love her faithfully for ever. At a formal ball, Siegfried dances with many princesses, but rejects all of them. He loves Odette. Then

the magician enters with his daughter Odile, who is disguised to look like Odette. She dances with Siegfried, he declares his love, and they taunt him with their trick. Odette tells Siegfried that the only way to break the spell is for her to drown herself. Siegfried vows to join her.

PHYSICAL SKILLS
Hitting The Target

Play and Learn

Recipe for Sugar Mice Prizes
1 tablespoon icing sugar; 1 egg white; few drops cochineal; liquorice strips, peanuts, glacé cherries for decoration. Whisk egg white, mix with sieved icing sugar and a few drops of water and cochineal. The mixture should be firm enough to mould with the hands. Mould the head and body as one shape and then let your child add peanuts for ears, pieces of cherry for eyes and liquorice strips for tails.

An aiming game
There are all kinds of games that you could set up at home to encourage aiming, rolling and throwing. You can roll balls down a ramp and through a cardboard archway, or a good game for improving young children's aim is to line up a variety of non-breakable containers and then see how many times your child can throw a "ball" (preferable to use a bean bag or ball of wool with very young children) into each container.

Telling a Story

David's stall
David's school was holding a fête. The teachers needed some money to buy the children a climbing frame for the playground. So they hoped that lots of people would turn up and pay money to have fun on the different stalls for the afternoon.

It was a lovely sunny day and the school looked very pretty with big posters and coloured flags everywhere. There was a hoop-la stall, a guess-the-weight-of-the-cake stall, an old clothes stall, a place where you could buy toys and books, a raffle with a huge box of chocolates for a prize, and even a donkey ride. You could sit down when you were tired and have home-made biscuits and lemonade too. David's dad had a stall. People had to aim darts at a dartboard and if they hit a high number they won a prize.

David felt very important because his father had helped him set up his own stall. David's stall was a bucket of water with a silver coin at the bottom. People had to drop their coins into the bucket and try and cover the coin at the bottom completely. If they did they won the coin as a prize, but if they didn't then the school kept the coin and all the other coins that missed. Lots of children wanted to have a go and David was very busy watching the coins sinking down through the water and paying up if anyone managed to cover the silver coin. He had so much to do that he hadn't even had time to go and get himself a glass of that delicious lemonade.

Late in the afternoon a big boy came along and dropped his coin in. David watched it sink down and go "clunk" on the bottom. "Bad luck," David said, "you lost. Do you want another try?"

"I won, I won," said the big boy.

"No, you lost," said David. "Your coin didn't cover the silver one, so you lost. That's the rule."

"Well, I'm going to have it," said the boy, and he bent over the bucket. But just at that moment a crowd of people went by and one of them accidentally pushed the boy. There was a crash and a splash and suddenly, the bucket was empty and the big boy was sitting in a big puddle.

"You see, you should stick to the rules," said David as people came to help clear up. "You didn't win the money, and now you're soaking wet."

Study Box

Have a go
But has he got enough money? Make a small chart that shows how many coins each stall needs. Give your child fewer coins than there are turns. Hold the coins in your hand and work together to put the right number on the chart each time he has a turn.

Stall	Coins for a turn
Hoop-la	000
Rifle range	0000
Coconut shy	0000
Fruit machine	0
Candy floss	00

Note *The actual value of the coins is not important because your child is unlikely to understand this aspect of money yet and you may risk spoiling the exercise if you try to teach it. All the same, children usually prefer to use real coins in this kind of work.*

Telling a Story

Polly's present

It was Polly's birthday. She was four years old. Sam, her older brother, had given her a special present. It was a box and inside were two bats, one red and one yellow, and a bouncy ball. When Sam came home from school they decided to have a game.

Polly had seen people playing tennis on television and seen it in the park, so she knew all about the net and hitting the ball over it. (Relate to your child's experience of tennis.) First they cleared a space. Then they made a net with some string and two sticks. Sam made some rules about how they should hit the ball and where it could go, and then they started to play.

Polly had a lovely time. She wasn't very good at hitting the ball. Sam always managed to hit it over the string.

Polly giggled and the more excited she got, the more she missed the ball. Sam kept winning the points (one, two, three, four, etc) but Polly didn't mind because she didn't know too much about rules and as long as she hit the ball with the bat, she didn't care where it went.

Next day, while Sam was at school, she practised with the bat and ball. Her mum helped her when she had time. She even made special drinks for when Polly got too hot. That evening after school, Polly and Sam played again. What do you think happened? This time Polly won lots of points and Sam wasn't very happy about this, although they had a much better game. Polly couldn't understand why he was upset, because she still didn't know too much about rules. But she was learning!

Play and Learn

Ball games

Have a game outside with bats or rackets and balls, and make up some simple rules for taking turns, scoring points or winning prizes. Let your child suggest some of these rules. Have something that functions as a net, line or goal so that the ball can be "in" or "out". If you cannot play outside, play an indoor version with skittles or marbles or table-tennis balls. See that the rules apply to everyone who joins in. Point to examples of organized games which you have seen in action outside or on television. Try to get across an idea of what is fair and what is not.

Hitting balls

It's very easy to give young children bats and balls before they are ready to use them: frustration results. Stuff the end of a sock with newspaper and tie it with a long piece of string. Hang it from a door frame and give your child a rolled-up news-paper to hit it with. Such games help develop your child's ability to co-ordinate hand and eye movement and will also help in many early learning activities. When she is ready for rackets and balls, give her ones that are the right size. You can spoil your child's enjoyment and skill development by making her use equipment that is too big or too heavy.

Study Box

It's not fair

As children begin to watch sport on TV or take part in their own games, they will learn that what is fair in one is quite unfair in another. You could use this table to see how much they understand about the sports they are interested in.

Sport	Fair	Unfair
Tennis (doubles)	Either partner can play shot	Hitting on second bounce
Table tennis (doubles)	Partners must play in turn	Hitting table with bat
Football	Kicking ball in any direction	Handling ball
Basketball	Handling ball	Kicking ball
Rugby	Handling and kicking ball	Passing ball forwards

PHYSICAL SKILLS

At The Circus

Telling a Story

Circus in the park

Richard, Janet and David decided that they were going to play clowns in the park one afternoon.

"Hurray!" said Richard. He immediately started pulling his funniest faces and rushing around tripping himself up and falling over with loud squeaks before the others could decide how to be clowns.

"Do be quiet, Richard," said Janet in her bossy, grown-up voice. "We can't hear ourselves think, and anyway, falling over all the time really isn't very funny. It's not making me laugh."

"Nor me," said David, who was a very serious boy most of the time. "Real clowns can do all kinds of difficult tricks like balancing and jumping. I'm going to see if I can balance on that ball."

"And I'm going to practise turning cartwheels," said Janet. "Why don't you see if you can walk along that narrow piece of wood on the edge of the flower bed, Richard? I bet you can't."

So Richard had to shut up and try to do something really difficult.

David fell over first. The ball just rolled away from

him. Then Janet tangled up her legs and crumpled into a heap just as Richard fell off the piece of wood and landed on his bottom in the soil.

As they all sat there looking cross, they heard someone roaring with laughter.

"You've no idea how funny you all look," said Fred the park keeper. "You're all being so serious, but you have all ended up in a heap! Proper clowns, you are. I ought to be angry with you for spoiling my flower bed but you have given me the best laugh I've had for ages!"

Play and Learn

Dressing up

A clown makes a lovely character for a fancy dress party or for cheering up a long afternoon. Your child will need white flour for his face, lots of lipstick, black crosses over the eyes and a ball of Plasticine for a nose. A baggy clown suit can be made from an old sheet. To complete the costume lend him an old wig, or stick some wool around the inside of a hat so that it hangs down like hair.

A miniature circus
When your child has some friends round, they might like to organize some circus acts to put on for you. Help with the initial planning, to make sure everyone has an act. One act that younger children might enjoy setting up is the toys' tightrope/ trapeze show. Tie pieces of string tightly between two chairs. Then attach some small toys to the main strings using paper clips, sticky tape, loops, etc. As much fun will be had in the making of the act as in the final performance.

Study Box

Feeling and doing words
These sentences provide practice in using those words that describe feelings and those that describe actions. Encourage your child to construct sensible sentences using the picture and this chart as a starting point, then going on to his own ideas.

How we feel	Reason
We are **happy**	when the clowns **fall** over and make us laugh
We are **scared**	for the acrobats as they **fly** through the air
We are **amazed**	to see the jugglers **throw** their clubs into the air
We are **surprised**	when the tall clown **walks** past on stilts
We are **miserable**	when the circus **leaves** town

Index

The index contains entries for the Learning Skills, Play and Learn and Study Box sections of this book as well as for the facts and themes discussed with each picture.

Page numbers in *italic* type are references to the Learning Skills and those Study Box sections which aim to help children practise specific skills.

Page numbers in **bold** type are references to the stories and the Play and Learn sections. These include projects, games and other activities which will reinforce the ideas put forward in a particular picture.

Index

The publishers thank the following for their kind co-operation and advice on factual content, and for supplying reference: Circus Fans' Association of Great Britain; Gages Hard Courts; Netherlands National Tourist Office; Royal Opera House.

The publishers thank the teachers and children of the following schools for their help in the preparation of this volume: Maxilla Day Nursery Centre, Notting Hill, London; St James's and St Peter's Primary School, London; Edmund Waller Infants' School, London.

Executive Art Editor	Debra Zuckerman
Editor	Carolyn Ryden
Art Editors	Peter Luff
	Marnie Searchwell
Assistant Text Editor	Edwina Conner
Assistant Art Editor	Mustafa Sami
Researchers	Louis Callan
	Nicholas Law
	Alice Peebles
Assistant Designer	Mary Padden
Project Secretary	Avril Cummings

Four colour origination by Adroit Photo Litho Ltd, Birmingham
Two colour origination by Colourscreens Ltd, Frome
Typesetting by Tradespools Ltd, Frome
Printed in the Netherlands by Koninklijke Smeets Offset B.V.